ERIC JOHNSON

Provoke Life

How You Can Help Jesus Change The World

PLATYPUS
PUBLISHING

First published by Platypus Publishing 2023

Copyright © 2023 by Eric Johnson

All rights reserved. No part of this publication may be reproduced, stored or transmitted in any form or by any means, electronic, mechanical, photocopying, recording, scanning, or otherwise without written permission from the publisher. It is illegal to copy this book, post it to a website, or distribute it by any other means without permission.

First edition

ISBN: 978-1-959555-35-3

This book was professionally typeset on Reedsy.
Find out more at reedsy.com

*To Emma and Leah, my amazing daughters
who provoke so much life in me.*

"I have come to provoke life..."

-Jesus

Contents

Preface	ii
Acknowledgement	ix
It's OK Not To Be OK	1
Grieve For Christ's Sake	14
Lead With Your Need	26
Feast On God's Future	38
Build A Bigger Table	50
Turn From The Counterfeit To Receive The Real	63
Wage Peace By Wearing Love	75
Embrace the Danger of Difference	87
Rejoice When There Is Resistance	98
Final Thoughts	111
Notes	116

Preface

Have you ever read the Bible and wondered why 1st Century Christianity looks very little like the Christianity of today?

The unfortunate truth is that Christians are known more today for what we are against than what we favor. Many of those outside of the Church hold the perception that Christians are hypocritical, judgmental, partisan, and anti-gay. While most admire Jesus, those outside church walls find very little about the lives of Christians that look like the One you and I claim to follow.

The Church needs a vision to become again what it was in the 1st Century and who Jesus always intended for the Church to be. The Good News is that this vision has been with us all along. It is a vision that will call forth that which Jesus lived, died, and rose again to create within you and I and the rest of the world. It is a vision that will "provoke life."

The story of God's relationship with humanity across thousands of years tells of a God who is alive and active in the lives of God's people. We see this most clearly in the book of Acts, where healings, miracles, and even raising the dead seemed typical. People came to faith by hundreds or thousands and the Good News of Jesus transformed entire communities.

More compelling than the miraculous, however, was the quality of life promised by Jesus. When Jesus talked about His version of life, He wasn't just describing beating hearts and breathing lungs. He was referring to an existence overflowing with everything God intended us to have at creation. It's what Paul called "the fruits of the Spirit" in Galatians 5:

love, joy, peace, patience, kindness, goodness, faithfulness, gentleness, and self-control. Jesus announced in John 10:10, "I came so that they could have life—indeed, so that they could live life to the fullest." The breakthrough of the Kingdom of God the world had been desperate for had arrived in Jesus and in the community He launched.

After Jesus' ascension, His followers extended the invitation to this version of life all around the world. While divergent beliefs and divisive behaviors were common within this new community, they provided occasions for early church leaders to redirect this new generation of Jesus followers to what was good and true.

Paul wrote of radical equality under Christ. Peter proclaimed the hope we have in Christ's return. James levied a challenge to align faith with action. John elevated love as the primary pursuit of God's people. Each had a unique lens through which they viewed life as Jesus intended - true, full, authentic life.

For the first three centuries of Christianity, the number of people who embraced this life exploded. Over time, Christianity transformed into Christendom as governments and cultures took this life and turned it into a religion. The insurgency became the institution, shifting from the edge of culture to its center.

There has been a lot of good accomplished by the Church as an institution over the last 1700 years. The cost has been that the miraculous breakthrough of the Kingdom was replaced with the hierarchy of an institution and, at minimum, the result has been a mixed bag. For certain marginalized communities, the Christendom church has done more harm than good.

Christian author Brennan Manning said, "The greatest single cause of atheism in the world today is Christians who acknowledge Jesus with their lips and walk out the door and deny Him by their lifestyle. That is what an unbelieving world simply finds unbelievable."[1]

Of equal concern is the impact this turn has had on those within the

Church. It's not just the "unbelieving world" that finds the state of the American Church unbelievable. If you view the decline of church membership over the last 40 years as any indication, more and more are leaving congregations because they fail to find anything compelling. Many within the walls of the American Church have discovered what those outside have been saying for a while. Events like The Great Recession, the 2016 Presidential Election, COVID-19, and the racial unrest following the murder of George Floyd revealed an underbelly of ugliness in congregations likely present but hidden from many until now. The Good News has ceased to appear "good" to far too many.

You don't have to know the statistics. Just think about what church attendance in your congregation was 20 years ago and compare it to what you see today. It would be easy to blame a culture of busyness as the reason for the decline in participation, and you would not necessarily be wrong. But I believe that most people can find time for what is compelling and adds value to their lives. Fewer are finding engagement in church communities desirable or accessible. Others do not find congregations to be welcoming of them at all. Our individual and collective need for Jesus has not changed. Still, many no longer see congregational life as a place to meet those needs.

It would be easy to lose heart and hope in the face of this current reality, but you and I are not those kinds of people. We are a people who worship Jesus, the One who died and rose again. We are a resurrection people who believe that life can begin again. And not just heart-beating, lung-breathing life – but the true, full, authentic life Jesus promised. A life of ever-growing fruitfulness. A life grounded in eternal hope. A life dedicated to faith revealed by action. A life of love. A life of breakthrough that transforms the world.

What will it take for a resurrection of this kind of life? There are several ways to answer that question. Volumes have been written to provide answers. Entire movements have been built around living out the mission of Christ to be disciples who make disciples. Parachurch organizations and new church starts have launched to "turn the tide of our culture" towards faith in Jesus. Denominations have studied it, formed task forces, and launched initiatives to counteract the accelerating decline of the institutional Church. Like the Church's shift from the edge of culture to the center, the results have been a mixed bag.

In our attempts to bring people into the Kingdom of God, we have lost sight of what it means to live in that Kingdom ourselves. The Kingdom of God transcends the institutional church, and yet, for many, the institution is all they experience. You and I need a clear vision for what we are giving our lives to and what we are asking people to join us in, and it has to be more than a church service on Sunday. Jesus wants us to be more than just "church people," but most lack a vision for following Jesus beyond going to church.

Fortunately, you don't have to look far to see that clear vision. It's been hiding in plain sight for 2000 years. It didn't come from a theologian, a church leader, or a denominational edict. It came from the One you claim to follow, the One who was present as God created life, and the One who died and rose again so that this true, full, authentic life can begin again in every time and place. This vision comes to us from Jesus and will provoke life within us and through us in ways no earthly vision or strategy could accomplish.

Matthew's Gospel tells of how Jesus drew a following by calling His first disciples, then demonstrating signs of the Kingdom. By the time you get to Matthew 5, Jesus attracted a large enough crowd that He had to climb up the side of a mountain so everyone could hear him. We don't know how many were present, but it is safe to assume that it was a sizable number.

And on that mountain, Jesus would cast a vision for a new kind of community. A community that would embody the Kingdom of God. A community that would be a light to all the nations of the world. A community that would provoke life. We call this vision the Beatitudes.

The Beatitudes are nine statements describing who the blessed people are. When we think about what it means to be blessed, it usually doesn't look like what Jesus describes. And yet, it is the poor in spirit, the mourners, the meek, the cravers of righteousness, the merciful, the pure in heart, the peacemakers, and the persecuted who are blessed. God rewards each for their faith amid their circumstances. They receive rewards every committed follower of Jesus would desire. While worldly riches are never promised, an abundance of love, joy, peace and the other fruits of the Spirit described in Galatians 5 are made available to those Jesus names as blessed.[2]

But then Jesus turns to his audience and describes how they too will be blessed. Following Him, Jesus tells them, will provoke a response. They should expect to be hated, mistreated, and slandered. Those who lived counter-culturally for God's Kingdom received poor treatment. They would likely be no different.

It is critical to understand what Jesus is doing in this moment. By naming the people He considered blessed by God, He describes the characteristics of the community He was calling His disciples to partner with Him in launching. In making space for the kind of people Jesus named, this community would provoke a negative response. Jesus wanted His disciples to be ready for that.

But what's left unsaid here is that the negative response Jesus described would not be the only kind of response provoked. Every action has an equal and opposite reaction. When there is opposition, there is always support somewhere. Where evil is provoked, good is not too far behind. Where there is the threat of death, there are always signs of life – true, full, authentic life.

Jesus taught the Beatitudes to His early followers and made sure they were recorded for you to read because He longs for you to embrace them, live by them, and challenge others to join you in that living. The

Beatitudes are world-changing. Jesus wants to change the world, and He wants you to help Him. If Jesus didn't want that, He would have kept the Beatitudes to Himself. But He didn't, which means you have a role to play in His plan.

The purpose of this book is simple: to hopefully reclaim the vision Jesus had cast in the 1st century for the Church of the 21st century. For too long, Christianity in America has focused on maintaining its status at the center of the culture. The center of culture is a place of comfort and security, but it is not a place of Kingdom breakthrough. The response 21st Century American Christianity is provoking is not one of life but of privilege and authority. It works (sort of) for those who carry the label of Christian but not for those who desperately need Good News. It is why you don't see the Christianity today that you read of happening 2000 years ago.

Breakthrough looks like the Kingdom of Heaven breaking into your world and mine through real and tangible ways. The early church saw physical manifestations they called signs and wonders. They participated in the breaking down of societal barriers. They were known for being sacrificial in their expressions of love and generosity because of the love and generosity they believed Jesus had shown them. They provoked life and helped Jesus change their world. You and I have the same opportunity before us.

The Beatitudes present a radically different way to live out your faith than perhaps you've been taught in your congregation or learned growing up. Each Beatitude is a challenge to die to yourself, and I will talk more about what that looks like in the following chapters based on what Jesus likely meant by each one. I'll provide concrete examples of how you can reflect these values and offer questions for reflection at the end of each chapter.

My hope is that this book presents a vision for both how you can be part of provoking life in the world around you and how you can connect with the blessings of God as you begin to live the version of life Jesus has for you – one that is true, full, and authentic. You won't receive that life sitting passively for it to fall in your lap. It will be stirred up within you – or provoked – as you embrace the Beatitudes as the rallying cry of your discipleship.

Living out your faith, individually and with others, centered on the qualities Jesus names as blessed, will provoke life in you and provoke a response from around you. And while there is the potential of the negative response Jesus described, the response left unsaid is the response of life – the true, full, and authentic kind He promised to give. When you make space in your life, family, and church for who and what Jesus describes in the Beatitudes, you will join Jesus in doing what He ultimately came to do. You will provoke life. You will see 1st Century breakthrough become 21st Century reality. You will help Jesus change the world.

Ready to learn how?

Acknowledgement

While it is my name on the byline of this book, it has indeed been a collaborative effort.

First, I want to thank my wife, Laura, the love of my life, my constant companion, and my partner in ministry. She first heard of much of what you have read in our many late-night conversations about life, faith, and church. She was my first reader and editor. Her feedback and support have been invaluable.

Next, I have so much gratitude for my family of faith at King of Kings Lutheran Church in Lake Orion, MI, where I serve as pastor. I wrote most of this book on a sabbatical provided to me by the congregation. I was burned out from pandemic ministry, needed a break from preaching, and was craving a chance to put what God had laid on my heart on paper over the prior year. They saw the value of a time of creative rest and provided it with enthusiasm.

As this book took shape, it would have looked vastly different and far inferior to the final product without the time, energy, and honesty of my good friend and ministry colleague Rev. Jessica Harren. Jess ensured that what I wrote sounded like me and aligned with what she believed I believed. She pulled no punches in pointing out areas of privilege I was unknowingly speaking from and challenged me to be intentionally inclusive of all potential readers. It took tremendous labor on her part, and I am so thankful.

A big thanks to Andrea Holt, who edited the finalized manuscript and affirmed that it was ready to print. Her excitement for the final product invigorated me to push to the finish line and get this out into the world.

Finally, and most importantly, thanks be to God, for the glory of whom this book is written!

It's OK Not To Be OK

Blessed are the poor in spirit, for theirs is the kingdom of heaven.

Matthew 5:3

"I do not doubt you'll do very well at chaplaincy functions. The patients you interact with will feel cared for, and you will provide them with meaningful spiritual direction. But if I let you, you will keep these interactions at arm's length and not permit them to touch your heart. This experience will not change you, and the process will fail you."

I was stunned by the words of Rev. Bill, the man interviewing me for a spot in a Clinical Pastoral Education program. CPE is an experience every ministry candidate in the Evangelical Lutheran Church in America (ELCA) must complete. Program participants intern in a healthcare setting, providing spiritual care to patients alongside board-certified chaplains while engaging in weekly day-long classes with other interns. The purpose is to not only offer pastoral care experience but to bring you face to face with death, illness, suffering, and grief, forcing you to confront whatever baggage from your life that bubbles up.

Clearly, in the 90-minute conversation we had just completed, I had done an excellent job of demonstrating competency for the work while also revealing a flaw in my character. Bill saw a disconnect between my head and heart that would prevent me from being honest with myself, my fellow interns, and God. I would not be changed by the process, and I didn't know how desperately I needed that change. But it was clear to Bill.

As a CPE supervisor, it would fall on Bill to lovingly but sternly challenge me to connect how I thought I was doing (head) to how I was really doing (heart) so that I might experience the healing, grace, and love of Jesus necessary to function in ministry. I had all the knowledge and little of the emotion, and that was not sustainable.

At that moment, I had not convinced Bill that the connection between head and heart would take place. Fortunately, Bill took up the challenge and invited me to be a part of the program, and it was perhaps the most formative faith experience of my life.

CPE introduced me to a part of me I had avoided for most of my life: the part of me that was not ok. Out in the world, you and I can keep that which we don't like about ourselves hidden from one another. But, as we wait at night with our thoughts for sleep to come, catch a glimpse of ourselves in the mirror as we get ready for the day, or, as in the case of the patients I dealt with, lay alone in a hospital bed waiting for relief from what ails our bodies, we know the real us. We just don't know what to do about it.

Think about the times you've seen someone you know at the grocery store, neighborhood, or church, and they ask how you are doing. What do you say? Most respond with some version of "I'm fine." And maybe, at that moment, you are. But most people aren't really fine. There is a pervasive feeling of lack, dissatisfaction, and grief in our culture that life has not turned out as you and I had hoped.

You encounter people all the time who are not ok. They are desperate for life and desperate to pretend they already have it. On some level, you do this yourself, but, in my experience, those disconnected from church and faith often lack the spiritual resources they crave far more than you.

We want to believe that a congregation can be the place for those needs to be met. The reality is our churches are too often not places where it is ok not to be ok.

Churches expect attendees to show up on time, dress a certain way, think, act, and live by what is "normal." Church members may value conformity and show disdain for disruption, both in the worship service itself and in the overall life together of the congregation. For many people who are not ok, stepping into congregational life is a bridge too far, even when invited to the most welcoming of places. They spend so much time pretending they are "fine," and it is exhausting to imagine having to pretend in one more venue.

If you and I want to provoke life, we need to create spaces where it is ok not to be ok because Jesus says that, where there is the poor in spirit, the Kingdom of Heaven breaks in.

What does it mean to be "poor in Spirit"? Understanding financial poverty can help us better understand spiritual poverty. Just as it was in Jesus' day, poverty is a crushing force in our day. Despite so many good-hearted attempts to solve it, economic poverty remains a systemic injustice that has vexed leaders for decades. There is a lack of political will to do what is needed to ensure financial sustainability for those at the bottom of our economic system. As a society, we've decided that a certain amount of poverty is acceptable so that the others might have a superabundance.

Poverty is a problem for those struggling under it's weight, but it is also a problem for those fortunate enough not to. Poverty serves as a reminder of what our society has decided is acceptable. It reminds you, if you are not living in poverty, of how you are complicit in the poverty of others. Poverty is brutal to look at, and those not living through it would just rather not look.

In many communities in America, including where I live, poverty is well hidden. My community has a trailer park dwarfed by a giant landfill,

Section 8 housing obstructed from view by a cache of trees, and low-income housing tucked away far from the main roads. I don't think this was any one person's decision, but as a community, we have decided what we do and do not want to see so that we are not reminded of what we have accepted.

I don't bring this up to be partisan but to use economic poverty as an example. We keep poverty of all kinds at arm's length, including our own spiritual poverty. We hide this poverty behind well-manicured landscaping, smiling vacation selfies, and "friendships" with people who are little more than acquaintances. No one knows the real us because we've constructed lives that prevent real knowing. We become defined by our consumption. Our souls hunger for more worldly stimulation to avoid the crushing reality that we are spiritually bankrupt. And when someone asks how we are doing, we tell them we're "fine."

This does not sound like the blessed condition Jesus names it as. Poverty of any kind is not a blessing from God, but God meets you in however your poverty manifests. The blessing Jesus refers to comes in the recognition that you can only find provision and satisfaction in Jesus because you have no other options.

My experience of those trapped in financial poverty is one of deep faith. While the economic systems of our day leave them behind, so many have faith that God will not do likewise and share profound testimonies of God's provision.

The recognition of your poverty is the place where the Kingdom of Heaven truly becomes yours. Your head reconnects with your heart, giving you the ability to be honest with yourself about yourself. Jesus brings God's healing, grace, and love to bear on the manifestations of your spiritual poverty and you discover that it is ok not to be ok.

Spiritual poverty tends to manifest in three ways. The first is shame, the reaction to the experience of not being approved of or seen as enough. In the Gospels, shame manifested before Jesus' first miracle of turning water into wine.³ It was the cultural expectation that the groom's family pay for enough wine for a whole week of celebration, and this particular family was about to run out on the first night. Had this gotten out, great shame would have been cast upon the groom and perhaps threatened the marriage itself.

People feel shame when their lives have not turned out the way they had hoped and they see themselves as broken, failures, dirty, or less than as a result. The cause could be decisions they have made, what others have done to them, or even circumstances beyond their control. When the cause of shame becomes public, it impacts how the world views the one who carries that shame. Private shame can be a massive burden, and public shame can be of tragic consequence.

The second manifestation of spiritual poverty is guilt. Jesus encountered guilt when religious leaders brought a woman caught in adultery before Him.⁴ While there seems to have been no consequence for the man she had been with (an injustice prevalent both in that day and today), the expectation was that she would bear the consequence for breaking God's law. Her sinfulness had legal and social implications, so she would have tried to keep her actions hidden. The exposure would have been her worst-case scenario.

In a culture where we've embraced a mentality that "Nobody's Perfect" and "Only God Can Judge Me," it would be easy to think that guilt doesn't manifest. It seems, however, to have taken on a different form. Where, in Jesus' day, guilt manifested based on what a person had done, it manifests today based on what is *not* done. So much of the do-more, work-harder, get-better, or else culture we live in is grounded in the feeling that we haven't done or aren't doing enough. While guilt and shame often go hand in hand, they differ in that guilt is about behavior while shame is about identity.

People feel guilty about not spending time with their kids, so they buy more toys. They feel guilty for not achieving more at work, so they ramp up time on the clock beyond sustainable levels. In cases where they do something wrong and thus feel guilty, they avoid the person wronged to avoid an expected confrontation instead restoring the relationship and relieving the guilt.

The third manifestation of spiritual poverty is fear. Not the fear that comes as a biological response intended to prevent harm, but the fear that not being ok will be a permanent situation. Jesus encountered this kind of fear from a leper, who was unsure if Jesus would be willing to heal him.[5] This uncertainty was likely well-founded as lepers were outcasts seen as threatening ceremonial cleanliness. Cut off from God and community with little hope for a change in condition, the leper approaches Jesus in fearful expectation of another rejection.

Of the three, fear drives much of human decision-making. People hoard wealth for fear of not having enough. They fail to take risks for fear of potential consequences. They resist change and progress out of fear of the unknown. At the root of these fears is the fear of not being ok because the world is convinced that not being ok is something to be feared.

Shame, guilt, and fear seldom exist in isolation. In each of the three Gospel examples and how each manifests in the lives of the people you know, the other manifestations can also be found. Shame, guilt, and fear oppose the true, full, and authentic life Jesus promised to bring, but they do not manifest because of our spiritual poverty. Shame, guilt, and fear are the outcomes of resisting our spiritual poverty, pretending we are ok, and telling everyone we are fine. It is actually when we become ok not being ok that shame, guilt, and fear lose their grip on us.

The Kingdom of Heaven breaks in when you and I embrace our spiritual poverty. As counter-intuitive as it sounds, letting go of the façade becomes a blessing to us. Jesus sets us free to be honest with ourselves and with others about ourselves. The humility, honesty, and authenticity of this stance proclaims to the world that it is ok not to be ok. And this stance will provoke life.

We know this to be true because there were times when Jesus was not ok, yet still, the Kingdom of Heaven broke through. After a particularly exhausting season of ministry where He fed thousands and battled with Pharisees, Jesus went to the region of Tyre looking for a break.[6] Jesus entered the house hoping to be alone, and He was not having his best day. The mother of a demon-possessed young woman approached him and begged for healing for her daughter. Jesus initially sent her away because He had come first for the Jewish people, and she was not Jewish.

The woman, perhaps recognizing how out of character this was for Jesus, pressed Him to consider her plight. While her daughter was not one of the "children" Jesus was focusing on, she reminded Jesus that her daughter also belonged to God and deserved consideration. Snapping out of the fog of exhaustion, Jesus agreed and healed the girl.

This is a troubling story. It isn't easy to believe that Jesus would turn anyone away, and many have attempted to explain why. We forget that Jesus was not only fully God but also fully human. He got angry, cried in joy and sorrow, and experienced weariness. The most straightforward expectation for what happened is that Jesus was not ok at that moment. This woman made space for Him, and the Kingdom of Heaven broke in.

Because Jesus knows what it is like not to be ok, He meets you when you are not ok. In this meeting, He brings healing, grace, and love to your shame, guilt, and fear. Jesus restores you and sends you back into the world. He did this for the family for whom He turned water into wine, the woman caught in adultery He did not condemn, and the leper He made clean. He revealed in their lives and yours that it is the character of God to embrace us when we are not ok. At the Cross and Resurrection, Jesus sets us free to embrace others when they are not ok.

Creating space where it is ok not to be ok provokes life because it brings people into a relationship with the same healing, grace, and love you received. So many have resigned themselves to a life of managing the impact of shame, guilt, and fear. It is an exhausting way to live, yet it is the only way they know. Jesus has a version of life for them that is so much better. He is calling you to join Him in provoking that life in them, and He has shown you the way in His healing of the woman with the bleeding issue.[7]

Imagine being cut off from everyone you love and everything familiar to you. Imagine not being permitted to return, to live with your spouse, hug your children, and worship with your community until you receive a clean bill of health and the endorsement of a religious leader. Imagine having to scratch out an existence, worrying about where your next meal was coming from because you had spent all the money you had trying to get well, and it had all been for nothing. Imagine this going on for over a decade.

This is what it was like for the woman with the bleeding issue Jesus encounters in Mark 5. This woman had suffered a great deal physically, emotionally, and spiritually for twelve years. The religious implications of her bleeding disorder would have labeled her ceremonially unclean, cutting her off from the world she knew. She had heard of Jesus' power to heal, and despite the crowd following him, she forced her way in to merely grab His cloak. She was cured of her condition in an instant, as power went out from Jesus and into her body.

While Jesus met her immediate need, He sensed additional assistance was necessary. He turned to look for who had touched Him. The disciples, seeing the crushing mass of people trying to get to him, retorted, "Uh, Jesus, *everyone* is touching you." The woman came forward, likely filled with shame, guilt, and fear for exposing a rabbi to her ritual uncleanness, and told Jesus "the whole truth," to which He declared her healed.

I find Mark's use of the phrase "the whole truth" captivating. Not just the truth that she touched Him or that the bleeding stopped, but the *whole* truth—all of her issues. I can imagine this conversation lasting longer than the few moments it seems to take up in the narrative. While this woman needed Jesus' cure, she really needed His healing. The bleeding may have ceased in her body, but her soul was also wounded.

Perhaps this woman sat at Jesus' feet, pouring out of her heart the toll years of trauma, loneliness, anger, and frustration had taken on her. As she shared, Jesus made space for her pain and anguish and helped her name, process, and make meaning around her ordeal. In doing so, He not only provided her with a physical cure but healed her spiritually and emotionally.

And it was not as if Jesus didn't have somewhere to be. The synagogue leader named Jairus, a man of status in the community, had summoned Jesus. This man's daughter was dying. He pleaded with Jesus to get there before it was too late. And yet, here is Jesus, being fully present with and listening to a woman of no standing as crucial minutes and maybe even hours passed. Despite the vital mission Jesus was on, He prioritized the needs of the person in front of Him.

I learned ministering in a healthcare setting through my CPE program that physical ailments are not all people bring with them when they land in the hospital. Time and time again, I would visit patients who would put on a brave face and tell me about their condition and prognosis. I would offer to pray for healing, thinking that would close our conversation.

It was amazing how many times the real discussion happened after we said, "Amen." It was as if the power of the presence of Jesus through our prayer broke down the facade. I know those conversations likely did not have the same impact as the one Jesus had with the bleeding woman, but I always walked away convinced that some degree of healing had taken place for that patient.

One downfall of Sunday-centric Christianity is that there is little space for people who aren't ok to not be ok. There is no space in a church service for the kind of interaction Jesus had with the bleeding woman or I had numerous times with patients on the hospital floor. The outpouring of ordeal doesn't happen during a worship set, a sermon, or even at the communion table. If you worship in a tradition that utilizes the altar call, *maybe* it can happen there. My experience is that the people who show up at the altar one Sunday are often back in the same place the next, so even that isn't effective.

So much of the focus of our mission is on producing church services and maintaining institutions. But, in a culture where so many carry shame, guilt, and fear, space to tell "the whole truth" and share the ways they are not ok is perhaps what the world needs most from us as followers of Jesus.

What if the church stopped trying so hard to tell its story and started asking those disconnected from church and faith to tell theirs? What if we were known as people willing to listen to "the whole truth" no matter how it challenged our preconceived notions about the world? What if we listened to the stories of people in poverty, even if it challenged us to examine our complicity? What if we listened to the stories of the addicts, even if their stories of addiction made us uncomfortable? What if we listened to the stories of members of the LGBTQIA+ community, even if it pressed us to examine our theology of human sexuality critically? What if, amid our busyness, we prioritized the healing of those in our neighborhoods and networks, making space for them to share the impact of whatever ailed them physically, emotionally, or spiritually?

I knew of an ELCA campus ministry who would begin each year by setting out a couch in the main quad with a sign that read "Tell Me Your Story." It was an open invitation to any student to share any aspect of their life and journey with a ministry leader. The conversation would last minutes or sometimes more than an hour. Occasionally follow-up conversations were scheduled. Every once in a great while, someone joined the campus ministry from this effort.

But this was not a marketing strategy. It was an intentional effort to make space for people to share "the whole truth" and to be a space where shame, guilt, and fear could be offloaded. The goal was not to attract students to a worship service but to provoke life on campus by letting the world know that it is ok not to be ok because the Kingdom of Heaven was near and available.

Changing the world starts with listening for what needs to change, first in your life, then in the lives of those God brings to you. As you become comfortable with how you aren't ok and address the shame, guilt, and fear you carry, you will more easily welcome others who aren't ok either. Making space for them to share "the whole truth" will initiate healing within them as the Kingdom of Heaven breaks through for them and you to receive.

I experienced this first hand in the wake of a local tragedy that garnered national attention. I live just south of Oxford, MI, a town recently touched by the national epidemic of school shootings. Because of the proximity of my community and Oxford, the impact here was significant. I took youth from my congregation to a healing event at another church and made space for them to share whatever they felt. At the end of our conversation, one of our youth, whose family has been members of a few churches in his life, said I was the first pastor to understand what it was like to be a teenager.

I'm not sure how true that is, given that I'm almost 42 at the time of this writing. Being a teenager over 20 years ago seems to be a lot different than being a teenager today. I also don't think I said anything remarkable during our time together. But as we talked and prayed, the power of the presence of Jesus brought a bit of healing to a fearful and anxious kid. It probably didn't change his world, but perhaps it gave him a bit of comfort and peace for the days ahead. It was worth it to make that space for him not to be ok, knowing that I was ok with that.

In 1 Samuel 22, David, the future king of Israel, was on the run from the current king, Saul. He wrote what became known as Psalm 142, a prayer that acknowledged before God that David was not ok, that he was afraid, and that only God could provide him refuge. In the midst of his struggle, God sent to him others facing similarly bleak circumstances. Over time, God rose up around David four hundred mighty men, who together became a community that would change the world of that time.

As you commit to discipleship that reflects Jesus' stance that it is ok not to be ok, you will help Jesus change the world by ensuring no one struggles alone. God will draw to you those disconnected from church and faith. You will experience the Kingdom of Heaven breaking into their lives as you make space for them to share "the whole truth" and find healing from the impact of their shame, guilt, and fear. And you will come to terms with your poverty of spirit and take hold of the Kingdom of Heaven for yourself.

APPLICATION

What you can do: You don't need a CPE program to embrace your spiritual poverty. Over the next week, sit with a journal and write down ways you think you aren't enough (shame), areas of your life you don't believe you've done enough (guilt), and the resources of which you don't have enough (fear). Find someone you trust to share that with, and encourage them to share their responses with you.

What your church can do: Every congregation needs to prioritize equally what happens on Sunday morning with creating points of community and connection beyond Sunday for existing members and those not connected. This could look many different ways, but there MUST be space for people to not be ok. That does not mean worship is not essential or a priority, just that Sunday church services are consuming a disproportionate amount of resources for their impact in helping Jesus change the world.

Discussion Questions:

1. Who in your life knows your shame, guilt, or fear?
2. Who do you know that is not "ok?" How might you make space for them to share "the whole truth" with you?
3. What opportunities does your church provide to make space for those who are not ok? What options could your church create?

Grieve For Christ's Sake

Blessed are those who mourn, for they will be comforted.

Matthew 5:4

I remember the first funeral I officiated. I was serving in campus ministry and preparing to start seminary. An acquaintance of mine approached me with the request on behalf of a friend whose college-aged daughter had died by suicide. I had never met this woman nor did she attend the college where I ministered, but the acquaintance knew there would be many young people in attendance and thought of me as someone they could relate to. I didn't even know if I was allowed to officiate a funeral without being ordained (I thought it was like weddings). Talk about the deep end of the pool.

I've performed a number of funerals in the years since, for parishioners and the public, in my church, and in funeral homes. I even led a funeral service in a park. A funeral is probably the most meaningful act of my role as a pastor. That may sound morbid, but grief is powerful and, when permitted, brings us to a place of raw honesty about what it means to be human.

The single unifying quality of humanity is that we all will die one day. Death strips away all illusions of grandeur we might have about ourselves. No matter how great we are, we will die. Everybody dies.

While the presence of death as part of the human experience is a tragedy, I have witnessed profound experiences of the presence of God amid human grief.

What troubles me as a pastor preparing for a funeral is when the family acts like the person isn't dead. What I mean is that they seem to do everything possible to avoid grief. I see this in families that push for the funeral to function more as a celebration of life. I get the impulse to focus on the deceased's virtues, and I've heard numerous loved ones say, "They would not want us to feel sad."

But we *are* sad when someone dies. We can't help it. Sadness overwhelms us when a life is lost, no matter how natural the circumstances. While I understand the impulse to minimize sadness, pretending not to be sad helps no one.

I experienced a version of this earlier in life. The summer after my sophomore year of high school, my best friend was killed in a car accident. He was the only child of parents I had come to know well. The whole thing was devastating, but I didn't know how to grieve the loss. I didn't know what to feel or how to process it. I never once cried.

It got to the point where my parents suggested I see a therapist, a suggestion I immediately shot down (I've learned a lot since then and recommend everyone see a therapist at some point in their life). To this day, I am not overly emotional, and I think on some level, holding grief at arm's length at 15 years old might have hindered my ability to access my emotions as an adult.

Even at funerals where the tears flow, sadness is acknowledged, and the reality of loss is embraced, grief still does not often get its due. Our culture puts a time limit on grief. Life will never be the same again, but the world expects the grief-stricken to get on with life anyway.

We treat grief as a linear process that ends eventually, and we prefer that it happen sooner rather than later. The grief of others makes us uncomfortable, perhaps because it brings our mortality and, therefore, the futility of many of our pursuits into focus – realities we would rather not face. It's like grief is some disease we don't want infecting us.

The psychology community defines grief as "the anguish experienced after significant loss, usually the death of a beloved person." It can also "take the form of regret for something lost, remorse for something done, or sorrow for a mishap to oneself."[8]

Grief isn't only expressed in response to death. Grief is an appropriate response whenever our life does not turn out the way we hoped, when we've done something or left something undone that harms us or others, or when we face some unexpected threat. The root causes of shame, guilt, and fear discussed in the previous chapter are natural sources of grief.

These create a heaviness or burden we feel over the state of our lives or our world, as though something we once had or were meant to have has been lost. We often carry these burdens without realizing or acknowledging it, but our lack of awareness or acceptance does not prevent the impact of our grief.

Our treatment of grief over death is a microcosm of how we view grief in any area of life. If you don't feel permitted to grieve the loss of a loved one fully, how will you grieve the gap between your expectations for life and life's reality? How will you grieve the sins you commit against God and your neighbor? How will you grieve that sickness, suffering, and death will eventually come for you, if it has not already?

I am not suggesting we dwell perpetually in these realities, nor do I believe it is healthy to dwell perpetually on the loss of a loved one. The promise we have in Jesus is that where there is death, there is always resurrection. Whether it is the New Creation or a new opportunity rising out of the ashes of the old, life will begin again! This is the Gospel we confess as followers of Jesus.

I am proposing that grief plays a critical role in the true, full, authentic life Jesus came to bring, and grief plays an essential role in provoking that life in others. When we allow ourselves to grieve and make space for others to grieve, whether that grief is the result of death, sin, mistakes, disappointments, or failures, life is provoked as those who mourn are comforted by Jesus' presence. Their grief, and ours, forges a connection to God's grace. If we allow it, grief can help change the world, so Jesus wants you and I to grieve ... for Christ's sake.

The truncated and sometimes optional expression of grief in our culture is utterly foreign to the culture of the Bible. To grieve in that time was a fully embodied experience. Mourners would behave in ways those with today's privileged sensibilities would find distasteful. Weeping and wailing, tearing clothes, and lying prone on the ground in times of grief were standard practices, as was the hiring of "professional mourners" to stir up even greater expressions of grief. Grief may not be a disease, but it certainly can be contagious.

These expressions of grief were not just appropriate in response to death. At different times in the Old Testament, God calls the people to mourn over what they had become as a nation. Israel's sinfulness and rejection of God's laws had wrought devastation in the land. Through the prophet Jeremiah, God instructs the people to hire the "best trained" mourners to lead them in sobbing over the death and destruction that were natural consequences of human brokenness.[9]

Our sin has real consequences to both our relationship with God and our relationships with people, and those consequences can and should be grieved if we are to move forward into the true, full, authentic life Jesus came to bring and provoke that life in others.

But just as it is today, some of Jeremiah's audience met the call to mourning with alternative reactions, instead relying on the worldly assets of knowledge, strength, and wealth to bring them comfort or insulate them from what needed grieving. God, through Jeremiah's words, tells them not to boast in what they possess.

Unfortunately, rather than facing reality, those who had benefited from the status quo sought human answers to the state of the world. God would have no part of this. God did not value their knowledge, strength, and wealth and saw those as no solution.

To the educated, who might say, "We know better," God said, "Be better." To the warriors saying, "We will do more," God said, "Do right." To the rich, who would say, "We lack nothing," God said, "I am everything you need." The only boasting that should have happened in Jeremiah's day was a boasting about knowing the Lord and God's kindness, justice, and righteousness.

What God said to the people through Jeremiah, God could just as easily say to us. The temptation is strong to look to our intellect, might, and riches as the solution to humanity's problems. These are assets given to us by God to steward, and they can help us. But our problems exist because we want to be gods of our own lives as individuals and as a people. You and I believe we know what kind of life we should possess, how we should act towards others, and what it is we are entitled to. When that inevitably goes badly for us, we look to these assets as the means to sustain us instead of realizing that our lives are unsustainable unless we surrender to the One who gave them to us in the first place.

To be clear, death, suffering, division, racism, ableism, fatphobia, sexism, homophobia, violence, nationalism, poverty, and every other societal ill exists because humans have decided we know better than God. Whether you believe the Garden of Eden narrative is literal or figurative doesn't much matter. Adam and Eve wanted to be like God and thought they could handle the knowledge of good and evil. They were wrong, and paradise was lost. If you and I had stood in their place, we would have made the exact same decision, and that is something we can and must mourn if we want to find our way back to life and provoke that life in others.

Grief is so critical to provoking life that even Jesus grieved. You would think that Jesus, the incarnate God in the flesh, would not need to grieve. Out of anyone who ever walked the earth, Jesus knew the whole story and how it would end. He knew of the promises in Revelation 21, of the New Heaven and New Earth, where God would dwell with humankind for all eternity, where every hurt would be healed, and where every tear would be wiped away. Jesus knew God would restore creation as God intended because Jesus was present at the beginning and saw the playbook.

And yet, Jesus grieved. He wept when Lazarus died. Jesus mourned over the lack of faith He found in Jerusalem. He cried out when the sin of the world rested on His shoulders at the cross. Jesus grieved because future hope does not diminish present sadness. To deny sadness exists would be to deny that you need a savior. And because Jesus loves you so much, He grieves when you grieve.

There is much you and I could grieve right now if we allowed it of ourselves. Many of those disconnected from church and faith could grieve if they felt they had permission. Life has not turned out for many the way they had hoped. Some have made messes of their lives and do not know how or if they can fix them. For others, circumstances have conspired to rob them of the life they see others living. All see time ticking and resources dwindling.

Jesus wants to meet them in that place, bring resurrection where there is death, and change lives and the world. You can't gain the new until you have grieved what you lost and the role you might have played in losing it.

You and I grieve, and make space for grieving, not just out of sadness, although we can be sad. We grieve for Christ's sake. We grieve as a way of acknowledging that our intellect, strength, and wealth are no match for the brokenness we see in our lives and our world. We grieve so that Jesus may come near and return to His rightful place on the throne of our lives. Funerals are such meaningful ministry because Jesus is present in grief and brings comfort. And when Jesus is present, He changes the world.

God shows us through the prophet Joel what a grieving process that provokes life can look like. In Joel 2:10, God proclaims judgment on Israel for breaking covenant relationship with God. But God also presents an alternative. If God's people were to gather together to grieve what they had done, individually and collectively, and return to the Lord the way a prodigal child returns to their parents, God would be quick to forgive and call the whole thing off. God would restore them, and they would not be without the comforting presence of God in their lives, even though God would be justified in revoking that presence. So great is God's love for you that God not only forgives you but comforts you in your grief brought on by your shame, guilt, or fear.

I don't believe there is one "right" way to grieve, whether our grief is rooted in death, sin, or change. Because we live in a world that makes so little space to grieve and demands that we move on quickly from grief, many don't know where to begin, just as I didn't when my friend passed away. A good first step might be to merely acknowledge the grief we feel - the burden and heaviness we are carrying. While funerals serve as a space where that acknowledgment of grief can happen, we lack culturally-acceptable spaces where we feel free to acknowledge grief or the sins we've committed, the mistakes we've made, and the disappointments we've been dealt.

A communal expression of remorse and repentance is what the Church's traditional liturgy is trying to get at in the Order of Confession and Forgiveness. I don't think that goes far enough, and if the only time we spend in confession is in worship on a Sunday, I don't think that's enough, either. Martin Luther taught that one's whole life as a Christian should be one of repentance, and grief over sin is a necessary aspect of the life change repentance brings. You won't change unless you know you need to change, and with the knowledge of a need for change comes a degree of emotion over how you got here in the first place.

However, that change does not come from rigid legalism or demand. The Apostle Paul writes in Romans 2 that it is God's kindness that leads you and I to repentance.[11] Jesus promised that His Kingdom is available on the other side of repentance, the Kingdom described in Revelations 21[12] where everything that was and is wrong in your life and your world will be made right again, the way it was intended to be at the dawn of creation. While this hope may feel a long way off, it is a hope that can lead us through our grief as we acknowledge the burdens we carry, the cause of those burdens, and the need for Jesus to bring us comfort and move us towards healing.

We can look to the 12 Step programs employed by recovery communities like Alcoholics Anonymous for a helpful model.[13] Steps 4 and 5 call for the addict to make "a searching and fearless moral inventory," confessing to God, themselves, and another person the "exact nature" of the wrongs committed. This practice goes far beyond a general prayer of confession and could not help but stir up feelings of grief. That grief would lead the addict to a place of readiness to ask God to remove those character defects and empower them to make amends where possible. Not only would the addict experience God's forgiveness, as the liturgy seeks to offer, but their attempts to repair wounded relationships might lead to restoration, as the remaining Steps intend.

Those in the 12 Step community advise that there is no timeline for these steps to be completed. They cannot be rushed, and there are no shortcuts. The only way out is through; while the word "steps" is used, the process is not linear. We cannot expect the prevailing culture of our day to change how it handles grief, but the Church certainly can change by making space for grief informed by the philosophy behind the 12 Steps.

As individuals, you and I need to reconnect with the emotions surrounding our current state, whether we got here of our own doing or by way of circumstances beyond our control. It is good and necessary to grieve that state, and in doing so, we make space for others to join us both in our grief and our eventual moving out of grief and into whatever newness Jesus is working out on our behalf. If we do not grieve, it sends the message to others that they are not permitted to grieve either, and we all stay stuck.

I learned this as a pastor leading a faith community and navigating the COVID-19 pandemic. While some congregations returned to public worship after the first few months, our leadership was uncomfortable moving in this direction. We remained entirely online even as some others around us returned to their buildings. We did not meet in person for over a year. I was convinced, along with our leadership, that this was the right decision and that we needed to make the best of a difficult situation.

I stand by that decision, but not how I handled it in terms of permitting myself to grieve that our family of faith was not together. Much of trying to do ministry digitally was a challenge. As the pastor of a small church, a lot of those challenges fell to me to solve.

Yet, in my public communication, I did not let on the toll this was taking on me. I was not even willing to admit it to myself. I powered through, expecting others around me to do the same. I knew on some level the toll not gathering as a congregation was having on some of my parishioners. I told myself there was no point in acknowledging how difficult this season was because there was nothing anyone could do about it.

In doing so, I fear I prevented some from grieving out loud or communally the toll the pandemic as a whole was taking on them. I know my failure to connect to my emotions during this challenging time was detrimental to my spiritual, emotional, and physical health.

Had I approached my grief and the grief of others with a 12 Step mindset, I would have spent time dwelling on the impact that leading in a pandemic had wrought on me. I would have been honest about that impact with myself, shared it with others, and taken it to God, not as a moral defect but as a present reality for which I needed the comfort of Jesus. I would have sought others out who were also impacted and stood with them in solidarity, multiplying the power of Christ's comforting presence. Even now, as I write this, I grieve the loss of what that experience could have been and am considering with whom and how I might need to make amends.

And yet, multiple truths can exist at the same time. While I did not create the space for grief that I wish I had, my congregation navigated COVID far better than many others I observed. We did not experience at scale the various fault lines that emerged during the pandemic in so many churches. We did not contend with vehement debates about mask-wearing, vaccinations, or public health orders. We did not see people leaving our church in large numbers because of the gathering restrictions we embraced. We were able to remain generally focused on our mission while participating with the Spirit to sustain our life together.

Why were we not impacted by the pandemic in ways so many churches were? My sense is that this was due to COVID being only the fifth worst event in the history of our congregation...and how our people had dealt with those past traumas.

In the twenty or so years prior to my coming as pastor, just about every bad thing that could happen in a church happened at King of Kings. A pastor died in office. Another went to prison for solicitation of a minor. Massive conflict emerged between a third pastor and the leadership cohort at the time, leading to that pastor's untimely exit. The church then remained without a called pastor for 5 years as they wrestled with the worship wars, the lingering effects of the conflicted pastorate, and deeply held dispute between factions over the direction and control of the church. This last traumatic event led to a painful church split.

It would have been exceedingly difficult to recover from just one of these events, let alone a nearly two-decade period characterized by ongoing trauma. However, in the period that followed the split, my predecessor and the leader who remained underwent an intentional process of grieving and healing. When I took this call in 2017, aside from the lingering financial challenges of the conflicted period, there were few traces of that period's impact. While it will always be a part of our story, it does not define our story because this church grieved for Christ's sake. A resiliency emerged as a result of grieving and experiencing Christ's presence in that grief that prepared this community of belonging for future crisis, including a global pandemic.

We live in a world where trauma comes in many forms. Death creates trauma. Failure creates trauma. Family dysfunction creates trauma. Disappointments create trauma. Trauma finds a source in any number of ways and there is no one right way to process it and move through it. Grief is certainly a part of finding healing from trauma of all kinds because Jesus has promised that those who mourn WILL be comforted.

Whether your grief comes from circumstances within your control (like the ways you fall short of God's will for your life) or circumstances beyond it (like a global pandemic), the key is to make space for your grief and the grief of others. When the world tells you to avoid or to limit your feelings of grief, it is actually the comforting presence of Jesus that you risk missing. But the only way out of grief is through, admitting the impact of the source of grief fully, acknowledging it to God and others, and looking for opportunities to repair whatever was lost or damaged. New life is available on the other side.

So grieve, and let others grieve, when life does not turn out as you hoped. Grieve, and let others grieve, when sin rears its ugly head. Grieve, and let others grieve, over future lack and uncertainty. Grieve for Christ's sake because you will find Christ's comfort in that grief. That comfort will produce healing and your healing will produce resilience. Resilience does not prevent trauma, but it does allow you and those for whom you make space to grieve to connect with the true, full, authentic life Jesus came to bring. And it will provoke that life in others.

APPLICATION

What you can do: The mindset behind the 12 Steps can inform your faith even if you aren't struggling with addiction. Spend some time reflecting on your life and world. What makes you feel sad? What happened to you, what have you done, or what do you fear? Allow yourself to feel every feeling stirred up, and share that with someone else. Then read Romans 8 and look for words of comfort in that text.

What your church can do: While a Liturgy of Confession is helpful, your church should not rely solely on that part of the liturgy to make spaces for people to grieve. Create additional space in worship for reflecting on grief over sin. Regularly lift the names of those who died in the last year and their families in prayer. Explore hosting GriefShare or another grief-focused program. Open your church building for funeral usage to those beyond your walls and be intentional about providing care and comfort for those who lost a loved one.

Discussion Questions:

1. Describe the last funeral you attended? Who died? How did you feel? How did others grieve that loss?
2. How do you currently practice confession? What emotions do you feel after realizing you've sinned? How long do those feelings last?
3. How open is your faith community to people's grief? What would need to change for you to become a place of great comfort?

Lead With Your Need

Blessed are the meek, for they will inherit the earth.

Matthew 5:5

It's fun to tell people I am the most humble leader I know. Of course, to claim to be the best at humility is one of the least humble things I can say. That's why it's funny.

The joke pokes at our culture's vision of humility that involves primarily outward behavior. Others view you as humble when you deflect credit, don't seek attention, talk about yourself very little, and think even less of yourself. In the extreme, the humble person is a bit of a doormat, taking what the world serves without protest. The idea of pursuing personal advancement, articulating preference, or holding fast to an opinion would not seem to align with how we think of humility.

We are prone to ascribe the label of "arrogant" to those who push forward with their opinions and ideas, those who openly seek to advance and progress, and those who aren't afraid to name their giftedness. Others have accused me of being arrogant, and, at times, it has been an accurate assessment of my behavior and required me to change. I try not to fear that necessary introspection, even though it can be hard. I have also found that the clarity of identity and confidence of self-worth I carry has also, at times, been confused for arrogance.

It may sound counter-intuitive, but clarity and confidence are critical to growing in humility. The more clear you are about who you are, the more clear you become about who you *are not*. The more confident you become in naming your strengths, the freer you will be to admit your weaknesses and flaws. These are intentional steps that the truly arrogant will never make. Clarity and confidence are one side of the coin; humility is the other. Humility without clarity and confidence is just self-doubt. In the anxiety self-doubt produces, we will look for unhealthy forms of validation in various ways.

I remember a birthday party we hosted for one of our daughters, who had requested a "Cake Wars" party theme. Cake Wars was a television show where contestants competed to bake and decorate cakes according to a particular theme. A judge would decide which cake was the best and closest to the theme, and the baker of that cake was the winner. I was asked to serve as the judge for the birthday party competition and told that I *HAD* to pick a winner.

See, my daughters have figured out that I'm no fool as a dad. When we have done competitions before, and my kids wanted me to pick a winner, they've seen me create different categories. For a drawing competition, I awarded one picture, "Most Realistic," and the other, "Best Use of Color." I'm generally not a fan of participation awards for kids, but I could not bring myself to elevate one child over the other or leave one feeling less loved, valued, and appreciated. Unfortunately, this was not going to be good enough for Cake Wars. My kids demanded that I pick the best cake at the end of the competition.

Of course, the validation from a Cake Wars victory is mild compared to the other ways self-doubt drives me and you to seek validation. While some will seek validation through self-destructive means, most just want others to view them as good, respectable, and competent. We often strive to curate an image for ourselves in the minds of others that we have life figured out, have a handle on what life requires of us, and are not people with need. What we often find, however, is that the validation of others never truly satisfies, forcing us to keep up appearances so that their favorable opinions continue to flow and temporarily medicate our self-doubt.

While the harm of this posture may not seem evident, it is a bit like a drowning man waving off the lifeguard trying to save him because he doesn't want anyone to know he never learned to swim. Life is hard and stressful, and so many are barely holding everything together. We've created a culture, at least in the US, where few want to ask for help because they don't want to let on they have a need. They convince themselves that relief is just around the corner, and they will eventually figure life out.

It is a far more destructive form of arrogance because it denies the state of need you and I can find ourselves in and causes us to reject the help at our immediate disposal. God created humanity in God's image. Because God exists as an interdependent community (Father, Son, Holy Spirit), the way you will fully bear that image is by existing in that same manner. Radical self-sufficiency enforces rampant individualism, permitting us to hide how in need of one another we really are. People are drowning because they seek validation in an independence they were never created to pursue and are incapable of sustaining.

Trauma compounds this validation-seeking. Abuse, neglect, or failure of any kind can multiply self-doubt and make it challenging to grow in clarity and confidence. If you did not receive healthy validation in your formative years, you are far more likely to seek it out in your later years, potentially in unhealthy ways. If mistakes you've made cause you to question your instincts, it will cloud your sense of identity and undermine your sense of worth.

That is why it is so critical for followers of Jesus to make space where it is OK not to be ok and where people are free to grieve for Christ's sake. Shepherding people through the effects of trauma to the other side can help them find the clarity of identity and confidence of self-worth needed to practice true humility. It is a ministry that is greatly needed. To be clear, there should be no judgment on those whose self-doubt drives them to seek validation in less helpful ways, whether that self-doubt is rooted in trauma or some other cause. It is the inevitable outcome of a lack of clarity and confidence.

It isn't common for clarity and confidence to be associated with meekness and humility. Still, it is only from a place of clarity and confidence that you are aware of all that you are not and, therefore, what you need from God and others. That awareness frees you to lead with your need, creating space for others to make valuable contributions to your life and your church and reinforcing that we depend on Jesus for true, full, and authentic life.

The perception of Jesus in our culture is one of humility and meekness. He embodies the description of the Suffering Servant[14], is referred to as the Prince of Peace[15], submitted to the baptism of John[16], and even surrendered His life to the Romans at the Cross. These Scriptural images of Jesus have been burned into the cultural consciousness of American Christianity regardless of any individual's religious affiliation.

And yet, undergirding Jesus' humility and meekness was a clarity of identity and confidence of self-worth. Jesus did not require the religious establishment's validation to proclaim that the Kingdom of God was near[17]. He felt free to assume the seat of the teacher and claim the identity of Messiah in His hometown synagogue[18], call out religious leaders on their home turf in the temple[19], and tell off Pilate just before He was crucified[20]. Jesus functioned in ways our culture might label arrogant if it was anybody else.

What made the difference? The easy answer is to say that He's Jesus. He does what He wants and is empowered to do so because He is God Incarnate. He can balance meekness and humility with clarity and confidence in ways that you and I can't because He is perfect and we are not. However, the idea that Jesus has access to clarity and confidence in ways we do not is patently false and denies the Holy Spirit's power to lead us to act more like Jesus through our baptism and confession of faith.

In His baptism, Jesus hears the words of God spoken over Him, "This is my Son whom I dearly love; I find happiness in him." This was Jesus' identity, and it is the identity you share by virtue of your baptism. It does not get much more clear than this: God finds happiness in you. Period.

And if God finds happiness in you for no other reason than because you are God's child, that becomes a source of confidence in your self-worth. You have worth because God said so, regardless of what anyone else says or thinks. As Paul wrote in Romans 8:31, "If God is for us, who is against us?"

Jesus lived out of clarity and confidence while also displaying meekness and humility. As Paul wrote in Philippians 2, He did not deny or diminish the fact that He was God but "did not consider being equal with God something to exploit."[21] This is a critical distinction in what it means to display meekness and humility. Jesus would have been well within His right to demand worship and devotion. He could have used His miraculous power to topple His day's oppressive religious and governmental systems and exact revenge on those who were complicit. He could have provoked death to establish His Kingdom through overt means.

But this was not His character. He came among a subjugated people suffering under the weight of Roman oppression to proclaim a Kingdom that was not of this world. He went into the desert to experience firsthand human need[22]. He served and allowed others to serve him. He called disciples to carry His message after He ascended to heaven. He traveled the countryside without a place to lay His head[23]. Jesus took on the life of a person with need so that He could lead with that need. In doing so, He showed us another way in which He would provoke life through us.

Our culture, and especially our church culture, has the wrong idea about humility. Because God is great and lives inside you in the Spirit's form, there is greatness inside you. You don't produce this greatness, nor does it exist because of you, but you can unleash it as you surrender to God's will for your life.

Humility, therefore, is not the denial of the greatness inside of you. It is about not exploiting that greatness for your advantage. Instead, meekness and humility are displayed by leveraging that greatness for God's will since God was the one who put that greatness there in the first place. It is walking in the clarity of your identity and the confidence of your self-worth.

Do you need Jesus to live out of clarity and confidence while displaying meekness and humility? Of course you do. Jesus said that without Him, you can't do anything[24]. Jesus also said that you would not only do what He had done, but you would also do greater works than that because He was returning to the Father and sending you the Holy Spirit.[25] The function of the Holy Spirit was to remind you of everything Jesus has said about you, bringing clarity of identity. The Spirit will also teach you everything you need to know, creating confidence in your worth. Both arrogance and self-doubt are traps and you need the power of the Spirit to free you from both.

I don't know about you, but I want Jesus to provoke life through me as He did when He walked the earth. I want to help Jesus change the world, even if it means I have to humbly admit how much I need Him to work in and through me to make that happen. I also know that without clarity of identity and confidence in self-worth, I won't be much help to Him or anyone else. Because God created me to bear the image of God through interdependent community, not only do I need Jesus, I also need you. And you need me.

As a pastor, I feel a certain amount of pressure to be all things to all people in my congregation. It isn't the fault of any one person or group of people but it is how modern Christianity has defined the role of the pastor. But it isn't a Biblical model for how a faith community should run.

In Ephesians 4, Paul lays out five roles needed for the growth and maturity of the Body of Christ: apostle, prophet, evangelist, shepherd, and teacher. Much has been written about these functions, so I won't spell all that out here.[26] Suffice it to say, each is distinct, with a certain temperament and skill set needed. No one person can occupy all five roles at once, but many congregations expect to take these five, roll them up into a single job description, and pay someone to do them for and on behalf of the congregation. This might be the most significant limiting factor of the church.

Early in my ministry, I felt a strong pull to serve in the role of apostle, which is the visionary leader dedicated to launching new ministries and leading people into God's preferred future. I was not wrong in thinking it was what my congregation needed, but I found that role exhausting over time. While I was competent to be an apostle, I discovered that my true character was that of a prophet. The chief concern of the prophet is not visionary leadership but listening in the context of community for the voice of God and discerning a faithful response. Prophets in the Bible spoke on behalf of God and made space for interpretation and response. The more I have tried to embody that role, the more life-giving leadership has been.

Clarifying my identity and knowing who I am also revealed who I am not. I am not the visionary leader who naturally draws people to myself for a cause. God wired me to be a prophetic voice, listening and looking for where Jesus is at work in the world and the church, and bringing challenge to the status quo. It is part of the reason I am writing this book.

And because I have growing faith in God's word spoken over me in my baptism that I am God's child whom God dearly loves - the same words spoken over Jesus at His baptism - I can own the identity of a prophet in ministry. I can also acknowledge that I am not an apostle, an evangelist, a shepherd, or a teacher, even though God may call me to function in one or more of those roles from time to time.

What I am seeing, as I lean into the clarity I have in my understanding of myself, is a far greater fruitfulness in the roles I am called to play than I would have experienced if I had tried to be something I was not intended to be. This has provided growing confidence to continue in this direction, even when there is pressure to conform to the expectations of others or the culture around me. And in humility, I must remember that this is not my doing, but is a blessing from God.

I am grateful for this clarity and confidence, but it doesn't go far enough. To provoke life, to inspire a meekness and humility that leads to inheriting the earth for the glory of God, I have to model it. The Church has to model it. And so, not only do you and I need to be aware of our need for God and one another, we must lead with that need.

Out of my understanding of the kind of leader I was and was not, I encouraged our congregation to shift governance towards a different version of leadership. In many congregations, the church council or elder board handles the business tasks needed to sustain the day-to-day ministry. Our leadership shifted towards a model that promoted discernment of vision and strategic planning while delegating implementation to those closest to the task. This freed me to lead from a place of authenticity, empowered the other leaders to own what we discerned as the next steps, and promoted greater participation from the wider congregation.

You may not be a pastor or church leader, but this example is still relevant because it speaks to the intentionality needed to lead with your need. If you are in need and want to see that need met, you must be willing to articulate that need to God and others. It would help if you also were open to receiving a response that is perhaps not what you hoped for or expected.

The Apostle Paul learned this in his ministry, and he recounts this to the church in Corinth in his second letter[27]. He talks about a "thorn in his flesh," limiting his capacity to proclaim the Gospel, make disciples, and build the Church. Paul believed that God would want him free of this thorn, so three times, he prayed that God would take it away. The response he received was simple. "My grace is enough for you because power is made perfect in weakness."

In other words, whatever this thorn in the flesh was, it kept Paul acquainted with how little his ministry and life depended on him and how much of it depended on God. Paul wrote that because his primary concern was building God's Kingdom and not his own, Paul would boast about his weakness so that Christ's strength would manifest through him. He would lead with his need and allow the work of the Spirit to change the world through Him.

Whatever your need, whatever you are lacking in or struggling with, it does you no good to hide it and pretend it does not exist. How God's power flows into and through your life is by boasting about that need. This has the effect of not only making the need known in your community so that others might come to your aid but also communicating to others struggling with the same need that they are not alone.

One aspect of humility is understanding that whatever good passes through God's hand and into your life is not just for you or about you. Leading with your need and embracing your weakness allows Jesus to be strong through you, and that strength blesses others.

There is immense discomfort and even fear when thinking about disclosing weakness and leading with need. When Jesus approached Peter to wash his feet at the Last Supper[28], Peter was deeply distressed. He thought it beneath the Lord to wash his feet, and perhaps he did not want to expose how dirty his feet had become. But unless Peter allowed

Jesus to serve him, Peter could not be in a relationship with Jesus because service is at the core of any meaningful relationship.

Jesus served Peter, and Jesus has also served us. As a result, we are free to serve others and to be served, to lead with our need, and to meet others' needs. This does not just happen in and through the institution of the Church, although we need one another as the body of Christ to fully reflect God's image in the world.

God sends us into our unique roles as spouses, parents, co-workers, students, and neighbors, but we still need one another. Some of the people you and I need aren't even in the Church at all and may never be. Someone does not have to claim the label of "Christian" for them to be a blessing to you and help meet a need you might have.

When my family moved into the town we now reside in, God made way for us to rent a home in a neighborhood with many small children. They became some of our kids' best friends and helped us to feel connected and acclimated to a new place. For a long time, we thought God had sent us to that neighborhood to share Jesus with those neighbors, and we were able to in various ways, but not one of them joined our congregation. We realized that while God had sent us to them, it was as much for our benefit as it was for anyone else's. We had a need, and God met that need through our neighbors for the five years we lived in that house. And we are grateful to God for it.

You and I can be so quick to want to serve Jesus and be on mission for Him that we forget we must first receive service *from* Him, and how He serves us in the day-to-day is through relationships with others. No one can serve you if they don't know what you need, and they might not think to ask. So lead with your need, even if it means risking their image of you.

Leading with your need means you first assess where in your life there is abundance and where there is lack. Perhaps you have a deep well of spirituality to draw from, but you lack relationships with others with whom you can share from that well. Perhaps you have knowledge and skills for helping others grow in their faith, but not a lot of time. Perhaps finances are an area of either abundance or lack.

Armed with the clarity of identity and confidence of self-worth, bring your need before God and your congregation or community. Also bring your abundance. Sometimes this means either an overt request for or offer to help. Sometimes it means simply showing up as you are. Obviously, it is critical that your community or congregation be a place that will receive you as such. At minimum, pray and look for safe people with whom you can be honest about your need. And, of course, be a person who receives others in the same manner.

You and I are responsible for growing in clarity of identity and confidence of self-worth and help others do the same. Someone plagued with self-doubt will not experience true, full, and authentic life. Empowered by clarity and confidence, the meekness and humility you show as you follow the example of Christ will make necessary space for others to gain clarity and confidence for themselves. As Jesus says, those who pursue this will inherit a whole world of relationships and influence.

APPLICATION

What you can do: There is greatness inside you because the Holy Spirit is there, but you are still in need somehow. Spend time reflecting on what you have in abundance and what you are lacking. Think of the physical resources you have at your disposal, like money, possessions, relationships, and energy, and more intangible relationships like faith, wisdom, knowledge, and experience. Look for those people who have in abundance what you have in lack, share your needs with them, and ask for help. Pray about who to approach, be mindful that your request is appropriate to the nature of the relationship, and permit them to refuse.

What your church can do: While some in your congregation are comfortable merely showing up on Sunday and consuming, most want to contribute in meaningful ways but don't know how. They aren't clear about their identity nor confident in their worth to the church. Discipleship initiatives that help your people work through their self-doubt and grow in clarity and confidence will go a long way toward building interconnected communities that reflect the image of God. Also, don't be afraid to ask those beyond the walls of your congregation for help, so long as you invite them into something meaningful and outward-focused, without expecting them to ever join you on a Sunday morning. Doing so will demonstrate a humility many of the people disconnected from church and faith won't expect.

Discussion Questions:

1. How have you previously understood what it means to be humble? Did this chapter challenge or even change your perceptions?
2. When was the last time you asked for help from someone or revealed a weakness to them? How did they respond?
3. What are some "thorns in the flesh" that remind you of your weakness?

Feast On God's Future

Blessed are those who hunger and thirst for righteousness, for they will be filled.

Matthew 5:6

What's the best meal you've ever had? What made that meal great?

I'm fortunate to be part of a family of excellent cooks, so I have had my share of delicious home-cooked meals, whether it was growing up at home, in my household now with my wife, or dining with extended family. But my wife's older brother, Corey, prepared a meal that sticks out the most.

Corey is a man of many talents and vocations, but the one relevant to this chapter is his ability to smoke delicious meat. It is both an art and a science for him. Every year, we gather for a week at his vacation home, and he prepares a smoked meat dish for one of our meals. He prides himself on what amounts to a 2-3 day process as he painstakingly crafts the right spice rub and puts the meat in the smoker until he achieves the perfect blend of flavor and tenderness.

One year, Corey decided to prepare prime rib for the extended family present. If there is food in Heaven, and there'd better be, I'm having Corey's prime rib every night. I literally could not get enough and nearly gorged myself on prime rib. I woke up the following day with meat sweats and a pang of hunger for leftover prime rib sandwiches at lunch. I may have had it for two other meals after that as well.

It's a meal I might remember for the rest of my life, but there is a problem: I've yet to be able to duplicate it since. Corey has yet to make prime rib in subsequent vacations (although he continues to make delicious meat dishes for us every year). On the rare occasions I've ordered prime rib in a restaurant, what they served me paled in comparison. Corey's prime rib left an imprint on me, effectively ruining me for prime rib from anyone else. When I have sought the joy of his feast from other places, the experience has left me wanting.

We live in a world defined by two competing realities. On one hand, Jesus has come, proclaiming and ushering in His Kingdom. The love, joy, peace, patience, kindness, goodness, faithfulness, gentleness, and self-control, what the Apostle Paul calls "the fruit of the Spirit," are available to us in Christ.

The true, full, authentic life Jesus came to bring becomes ours when we embrace the grace of God available in the death and resurrection of Christ. We see the beauty of the Kingdom in creation, in relationships, and in one another. It's so real, we can almost taste it the way I can still almost taste the pinnacle of prime rib I experienced years ago.

And yet, for all the beauty, we are surrounded by brokenness. I've spent enough time in this book unpacking the roots of that brokenness and its impact. The result of the presence of brokenness is that a hunger and thirst grow within us for the beauty that is the true, full, authentic life of Jesus. No matter how we might try to satisfy that hunger and thirst through pursuits apart from Jesus' version of life, we only really feast when we feast on God's future.

God hard-wired into us a need to consume with the intention that we hunger and thirst for that which God would provide. There are consequences when you do not consume what God intended for you. It isn't judgment or punishment from God but simply the natural outcome of disordered consumption. If you eat a super-sized meal combo every day, as was attempted in the infamous 2004 documentary *Super Size Me*, your body will begin to break down. If you overindulge in trashy, violent, or upsetting media content, it will impact you physically, emotionally, and spiritually.

I remember watching a reality cooking show where the host, a famous chef, would scream, belittle, and curse at the contestants for not living up to his exacting standards. At first, I enjoyed the show but noticed difficulty sleeping on the nights I would watch it. After a few episodes, I felt anxious whenever the host raised his voice. The last straw was, while he was in the middle of another tantrum, I felt my heart pounding as though it would burst from my chest. What I consumed was detrimental to me, so I turned it off and never watched another episode.

You consume, whether it be food or media, because you have needs, but what you consume might not meet those needs. Instead, you trick your mind, body, and soul into believing that what you consume is satisfying. It works for a little while, but you find yourself empty once again, and, over the long haul, you risk the repercussions of unhealthy consumption patterns.

But the problem of unhealthy consumption goes beyond food or media. The prevailing culture is built on a version of consumption that benefits us first. As I've stated elsewhere, I believe the root of human brokenness and dysfunction to be our ascent to the throne over our lives, a place only God is fit to occupy. As a result, we make most of our decisions through the lens of the self. We "consume" a version of life that we think is best, and this consumption is unhealthy and does not satisfy our hunger, thirst, and emptiness.

Because God created you in God's image, God imprinted God's Kingdom on your soul. Try to fill that imprint with anything other than God's best, and it will leave you wanting. God has effectively ruined you for anything less than the life and future God intends. You can search for it in many places, but you will only find satisfaction in feasting on God's future. Jesus promises fulfillment when you pursue the life and world He intends and wants to work through you to accomplish. That is what it means to "feast on God's future."

Through the prophet Isaiah, God implores humanity to reconsider on what we feast. "Why spend money for what isn't food, and your earnings for what doesn't satisfy? Listen carefully to me and eat what is good; enjoy the richest of feasts."[29] The covenant God was trying to draw Israel into was one of true, full, and authentic life, but they kept looking for that life through ways they thought best. You and I can act similarly in our pursuit of unfulfilling life and in that pursuit's resulting emptiness.

You will not find fulfillment in self-focused consumption. Your true satisfaction comes from consuming the righteousness of God. The words, works, and ways of Jesus reveal this righteousness. It is what God designed you to "consume." When you hunger and thirst for this righteousness, you will be fulfilled and provoke life as those around you see how your consumption has changed you. The shift you make to consuming the righteousness of God will bring transformation in and around you, and there will be others who will want that for themselves.

But what is the righteousness of God? The religious leaders of Jesus' day consumed a moral righteousness in their strict adherence to and promotion of their Scriptures. In His debates with these leaders, Jesus made clear that it was not external behavior alone that mattered to God. It was an internal transformation that indicated one was in right relationship with God. Today, that right relationship is how most Christians understand what it means to be righteous.

However, the righteousness Jesus calls you to hunger and thirst for goes beyond a personal relationship. Jesus has secured for humanity a better future in which *all* people are in right relationship with both God and one another. It is a future in which the world is changed, and Jesus wants you to help Him change it. In this future, the prisoners are set free, the blind receive sight, the oppressed are relieved of their burdens, and all of humanity will bask in God's favor. You will find fulfillment in this righteousness as you hunger and thirst for it. You will provoke life when you feast on God's future.

Imagine a world where violence, division, poverty, and suffering no longer characterize the lives of so many. Imagine a world of beauty, passion, creativity, joy, and unhurried rest. It seems lofty to even think about, and so you might be tempted only to give it a passing thought as you read this.

I want you to stop reading, put the book down, close your eyes, and imagine that world. Do it right now. I'll wait.

(For real. Take 5 minutes in silence and imagine that kind of world.)

Great job! Sitting in silence is difficult and not something to which we are accustomed. How did it feel to imagine such a world? Joyful? Exciting? Did your heart feel warm as you thought about what the future God intends might be like? The picture you imagined is part of what God intends creation to become. You have a role to play in that part of God's future. If Jesus showed it to you through the Spirit at work in your reflection, there is something in there that Jesus wants you to do.

Now, compare that to what you might have imagined if I ask you to reflect on the future you've wanted for yourself. Perhaps it was a future where you paid off your debt, lived in a nice house full of respectful and successful children, worked a job that made you feel significant and had a plan for a leisurely retirement. You shouldn't feel ashamed to want these things. It is the American Dream, and the promise of that future very minute of the day. But you are not promised that future, pursuit of that future as your primary motivation genuinely fulfilling. Feasting on God's future, a future in pursuit of righteousness, will leave you full.

Jesus was so convinced that His righteousness was the only truly fulfilling pursuit that He stood on a mountain in front of hundreds of people well acquainted with physical hunger and thirst and told them so. Can you imagine being there, perhaps not having eaten anything in days, and hearing the Messiah using a defining characteristic of your life to drive home a point? The response must have been visceral, yet the metaphor would have landed. "Hunger and thirst for the things of God," Jesus was saying, "and you will know a feeling of fulfillment you've never quite experienced before."

Of course, Jesus drew many detractors and lost more than a few followers because the promised future did not align with the one they wanted to consume. But this was, and is, good news. As long as life is about you and what you want, it is up to you to make it happen. You have to cook the whole meal yourself. Instead, Jesus is inviting you to feast on what He has prepared, and He does not need you to bring anything with you to dinner.

Scripture is full of metaphors using food and drink to describe how God sustains us by faith in a life of service. In John 4, He offers the Samaritan woman "living water" to quench her spiritual thirst. Soon after, the disciples worry that Jesus isn't eating, so they suggest it is lunchtime. He explains that His "food" is to do God's will. In John 6, after Jesus feeds the crowds miraculously, He calls himself "the Bread of Life" and challenges them to eat and drink of Him rather than just what comes to them from His hand. At the Last Supper, Jesus takes bread and wine to symbolize His broken body and shed blood.

Feasting on God's future, the one you imagined a few paragraphs ago, means allowing the pursuit of that future as the organizing principle of your life. Don't just imagine what it could look like, take action toward that future. It's the difference between picking at the food placed before you (the way a child might pick at their vegetables) and diving into the meal enthusiastically. When you embrace God's future in this way, the work you will do to pursue this future will be as natural as breathing. You will provoke life, and you might not even realize it.

This seems to be at the heart of Jesus' words in Matthew 25. Jesus was teaching about what would happen when He returned, and He told His followers He would divide the nations of the world into two categories: the righteous, who are His sheep, and the unrighteous, who are His goats. The sheep will receive a reward in Heaven, while He will send the goats to an eternity suffering apart from God.

The determining factor was how the nations treated those Jesus called "the least of these" siblings of His. Jesus named the hungry, the thirsty, the naked, the sick, and those imprisoned as those whose treatment mattered to Him - all categories of people the nations of the world in His day and our day are perfectly comfortable casting aside. It is a sobering passage, and preachers have used it to strike fear in the hearts of their listeners or have attempted to explain away as though Jesus really didn't mean it.

But notice the confusion in both groups. The unrighteous goats ask the king when it was that they didn't serve him. The problem was not a lack of service but a lack of service that made a difference for those who *really* needed it. They may have served those they were comfortable serving in line with the priorities and preferences they had for their lives. Meanwhile, the righteous sheep wondered when it was that they served the king. They lived lives where service of the least of these was the organizing principle of their lives - as natural as breathing. They helped *anyone* who came in their path.

Making this shift is hard. In fact, it is impossible to do it on your own. Going out of your way to serve those the world has cast aside is inconvenient and costly. At least, that's what you might think. You think this way because you are a goat, but Jesus can make you a sheep. You are unrighteous, but Jesus can make you righteous only when you hunger and thirst for it.

Out of that righteousness, you will orient your life on the priorities and preferences of Jesus. You will feast on God's future because you will see yourself as you indeed are: one whom Jesus has invited to dine on what He has laid before you - a life of serving and reaching the last, least, lost, and lonely.

You may wonder what will happen to you if you give your life away in this manner. How will your needs be met? This was apparently a question others were asking Jesus, and Jesus made the answer clear. In Matthew 5, Jesus pointed out the birds of the air and the flowers of the field. Neither needed to strive beyond themselves, yet their needs are always met and contribute to the beauty of creation. You are a far more beloved creation than those, so why wouldn't God attend to your needs in ways that exceed mere birds or flowers?

Jesus promises that when you seek first the righteousness of God, everything else falls into its place. You will have all you need without striving to arrange it yourself. You are free in Christ to feast on God's future. It is a future where the last are brought forward, the least find their place among the most, the lost are found, and the lonely are surrounded with love.

As you hunger and thirst for the righteousness of God, you will find opportunities to feast on God's future. You might begin to notice those society would cast aside, and you will want the goodness of God to come to them. The Spirit will make clear to you how you might serve them. It will be unique to you and the part of God's future the Spirit led you to imagine. You don't have to do it like anyone else. Just dine on the meal set before you.

Sometimes this means tangible acts of service, but the more time you spend with those on the margins, the more you become aware of the systemic forces responsible for their marginalization. Those Jesus named as the "least" of his siblings are often in that state for reasons beyond their control. Remember, righteousness is not about the right action but the right relationship. Our world is organized in systemically divisive ways, and many benefit from those divisions. Those privileged to be at the center as opposed to the margins can count themselves among the beneficiaries.

This isn't something to feel guilt or shame about, but it is important to acknowledge so that you can be open to the Spirit's leading for how you will use that privilege to serve. Your "cup of water to the thirsty" might be to stand against racial injustice publicly. Your "clothing of the naked" might be to advocate for better working conditions and pay for service employees. Your "visiting those in prison" might be to hire the formerly imprisoned. While well-intentioned, too much of what passes for Christian services does not require much sacrifice nor moves the world closer to God's future. It is an add-on to our lives, not the orientation of our lives. It's a snack, not a meal.

What truly provokes life and helps Jesus change the world is following God's command in Micah 6:8 to "seek justice, love mercy, and walk humbly." Do this in your family. Do this in your neighborhood. Do this in your job. Do this in your church. Do this in and with those in your network that the world has cast aside. If no one in your network fits that bill, find them while asking yourself how you ended up so disconnected from those with whom Jesus most identifies.

Doing justice begins by listening to the stories of those impacted by the various injustices in your world. So often, you and I are silent in the face of injustice simply because that injustice does not personally affect us or anyone we know. As soon as the face of someone we come to know and care about gets attached to that injustice, it is nearly impossible to ignore. The Spirit gnaws at our conscience, causing us to look for ways to pray, speak, and act in opposition to that injustice.

Loving mercy begins when you embrace the faithful love of God and then express the love of God to others. The Hebrew word for mercy here is "chesed" and imagines a love that looks and acts towards us with compassion. God has taken compassion on you and empowers you by the Spirit to share that compassion in the world. You can't love mercy and keep it to yourself.

Walking humbly with God begins by cultivating a lifestyle of engaging with God beyond Sunday. This happens through prayer, Scripture reading, and daily gratitude for God's blessings. Even as a pastor, my daily time with God is sometimes hard to come by. It's easy to say I'm busy and don't have time for that. But the days I spend 10-15-20 minutes alone with God are the days I am most aware of God's presence and most reminded of God's kindness.

It is critical that you refrain from doing this out of some legalistic or moral obligation because that will not be sustainable. Do this because it is the path to true fulfillment. It's the meal you can't recreate anywhere else. Finding a spouse, becoming a parent, succeeding at work, and retiring comfortably are all fine pursuits. They just pale in comparison to what Jesus serves up in the true, full, authentic life He came to bring.

Perhaps a way of thinking about them is as components of the meal instead of the main course. The prime rib dinner I sincerely enjoyed was not the only food served that night. There were potatoes, vegetables, wine, and dessert, all of which complemented the main dish but did not distract from that which was central. All were consumed in relationship with the primary focus of the meal: the prime rib.

Accordingly, every role you play is part of the feast God has prepared for you. Each role is a vocation Jesus sends you into to die to yourself for the sake of another. In your marriage, your family, your job, your school, your neighborhood, your friendships, your finances, and your retirement, Jesus is calling you to seek His righteousness and let that be what fulfills you, just as He referred to His being "fed by doing the will of the one who sent me and by completing (God's) work."[30]

That may feel like a lot of pressure, but Jesus' yoke is easy, and His burden is light. How do you know who to serve and when? The Parable of the Good Samaritan sheds a lot of light on this. Before telling the parable, Jesus is asked those same questions - specifically, "Who is my neighbor?" Rather than answering the question of who, He tells a parable describing how. While the ones Jesus' society deemed as righteous passed by the man beaten by robbers on the dangerous road, the Samaritan demonstrated self-sacrificing concern, care, and generosity. He likely did not set out on that road looking for someone to help, but when the opportunity presented itself, he took action despite his other obligations.

That is how God has created you to live. That is the imprint on your soul, to be that kind of person. God's future is one in which all of humanity conducts themselves in that manner, and when you take steps to align yourself with that kind of righteousness, it provokes life. You are helping Jesus change the world.

What made Corey's prime rib such a great meal was the love and care he poured out to make the meal happen. God in Christ poured out great love and care in creating you, redeeming you, and calling you to provoke life and help Jesus change the world. As Paul wrote in Ephesians, "You are saved by God's grace because of your faith. This salvation is God's gift. It's not something you possessed. It's not something you did that you can be proud of. Instead, we are God's accomplishment, created in Christ Jesus to do good things. God planned for these good things to be the way that we live our lives."[31]

Jesus is the one who sets the table, determines the menu, and serves the feast. God's future glorifies God and is for your good and the good of the world. That future is a feast, so dig in!

APPLICATION

What you can do: The image God gave you in the five minutes you imagined God's future did not come to you by accident. Return to that [p43 handwritten] image in times of prayer and reflection. Write it down and refine it, asking for wisdom about the role you are to play in that future. Share what you have written with others, and ask them to imagine their part.

[handwritten: world of God's beauty, passion, creativity, joy + unhurried rest]

What your church can do: Gather together to take stock of the community you live in and if your congregation's makeup reflects that community. If not, why not? What barriers would the last, least, lost, and lonely have to cross to be a part of your congregation? Recognizing that they probably will not take the first step, imagine how your people might step beyond those barriers, and take action on what you have imagined.

Discussion Questions:

1. What was the best meal you ever had? What made that meal great?
2. What was the part of God's future you imagined? [handwritten: peace + love]
3. Who are your community's last, least, lost, and lonely? How might you be in relationship with them?

Build A Bigger Table

Blessed are the merciful, for they will receive mercy.

Matthew 5:7

"I don't need you to tell me what you think I should do. I just need you to listen!"

One of the great blessings of my life is having a spouse who is very direct about her wants and needs.

I discovered this quality very early in our dating relationship. She had just started a new job and was struggling with one of her co-workers. Being the "supportive and helpful" boyfriend that I was, I believed it was my job to solve all her problems for her. So I would listen just long enough to diagnose what I thought the problem was and then turn my attention to formulating the solution I thought would resolve it, even if she hadn't actually stopped talking yet.

I do not recommend this in relationships.

After this happened a few times, she stopped me mid-solve, explained that she could solve the problem, knew exactly how she would approach the situation the next day, and did not really need my help. She needed me to listen, care, and relate to and with her in what she was going through.

What she needed from me was mercy.

There are many ways to define mercy, but the definition I most favor is mercy as the extension of loving friendship, care, and concern regardless of the existence of reasons, valid or otherwise, to withhold those from another. You show mercy when you enter into relationship with another despite all the reasons you might have not to be in relationship with that person. And you find there is mercy for you in that relationship, too.

Of course, those who have long been a part of the Church are quick to equate God's mercy with God's forgiveness. Forgiveness comes from God's mercy, but forgiveness does not express the fullness of God's mercy. Mercy flows through relationships, especially relationships that appear outwardly unlikely.

This is how Jesus operated. The Apostle Paul wrote in his letter to Colossians that Jesus is, "the image of the invisible God."[32] In other words, if you want to know what God is like, look at Jesus. Jesus did forgive sins, but His friendship, care, and concern for people went far beyond mere forgiveness. He listened to and cared for people. He related to and with them, particularly those on the margins. Jesus showed mercy by becoming friends with those everyone else had cast aside.

In Jesus' culture, and arguably in ours, a shared meal in a home was a sign of true friendship and acceptance. This was not only true for the person making the invitation, but also for the one saying yes. If you held a position of honor in the culture, you extended that honor to whomever you would share a meal with.

It was common in Jesus' day for rabbis, teachers, and prominent leaders to receive many invitations so that their presence in the inviting households would bestow greater status on that household. Those possessing greater status would also accept or reject invitations based on how dining with a particular household might impact their standing in the community. To be seen dining in a household of lowly status could do significant social damage to one seeking to build a following.

This is what made Jesus dining with sinners and tax collectors so confounding to the religious leaders of His day. They had no doubt heard of His teaching surpassing theirs in terms of authority. Some had witnessed for themselves His miraculous demonstrations of the Kingdom of God. They would have expected Him to court them for dinner invitations, only to find Jesus not only dining with sinners and tax collectors but even calling one of them to be His disciple.

What the religious leaders of Jesus' day failed to understand, and what the Church of today often forgets, is that Jesus' purpose was to reconcile all creation to God. All means *all*. Every human being that ever lived was in the mind of Jesus as He walked the Earth and hung on the cross. There is not one person who is outside of God's love, God's grace, and God's purpose. No one is outside of God's mercy.

The problem is that established religious systems do not do a good job of communicating this message. It does not take long for rules and regulations to be set, usually with good intentions and for good order.

But it also does not take long for those rules and regulations to draw clear lines of who is in and who is out, whose needs and perspectives are at the center, and whose are marginalized and ignored. In time, those on the outside stop looking in because they do not believe there is anything in the system for them. Tragically, they come to believe that not even God is for them.

Jesus encountered an established religious system that reinforced the human-created idea that God was for those who were ritually pure and religiously devoted. For the reign of God to break in, Jesus had to undermine that system by confounding expectations of who the Messiah would be, what the Messiah would do, and where the Messiah would draw His followers. Doing so would demonstrate that it was mercy and not sacrifice that God desired for God's people.

For Jesus to provoke life in the first century, He had to build a bigger table. To provoke life in the 21st century, Jesus calls you and I to do the same.

Religion isn't the only system that draws lines of stratification between who is in and who is not. Socioeconomics, family, education, and career can all create hierarchies of status. You and I tend to gravitate to those who are "like" us, creating comfort zones in which we can remain.

The longer we stay within them, the more rigidly the boundaries develop, and the more apparent the qualities of an outsider become. Defining what makes an outsider means it is easier to judge the outsider, and the more judgmental we act, the less likely we will engage meaningfully with outsiders.

Unfortunately, the Church in the 21st century has come to reflect this stratification. Sunday morning has been called the most segregated hour of the week in all but the rare cases. Rev. Martin Luther King Jr first coined this phrase to describe racial segregation in the Church, but the homogeneity he witnessed has expanded beyond race. Our congregations have great uniformity racially, socioeconomically, educationally, and politically. Congregations can serve as echo chambers of particular ways of thinking, believing, and living, to the detriment of their ability to provoke life in their surrounding communities, which, because of sheer size, often possess far greater diversity.

When the congregation in which you worship does not reflect the diversity of the community you reside in nor the diversity of the Kingdom of God, it makes it really hard to show mercy. You will see those who aren't like you as the "other" or the "outsider." You will stand apart from them, even in your attempts to serve or reach out to them. You might even be tempted to look down on them or see it as your job to solve whatever problem you perceive them to have.

It is a bit like the church that provides meals to the poor, but the church members who serve the dinner remain in the kitchen while the poor dine separately. Giving them a meal may seem like it solves their problem, but what they really need is mercy. They long for the dignity of someone listening, caring, and relating to and with them. If they are disconnected from faith in Christ, it will be the mercy of a relationship and not the filling of their stomach alone that will help them reconnect to the love of God that has always been present for them.

The gravitational pull towards the comfortable is strong, but remaining in your comfort zone is not good for you. It promotes spiritual complacency and robs you of the opportunity to be blessed by the diversity of God's Kingdom. Maintaining the boundaries that keep discomfort out is hard work and requires sacrifice, but that is not what Jesus wants for you. It is easy to blame the culture that surrounds the Church for the stratification within it, but Jesus came to break down those barriers.

You are called to be a part of breaking down those barriers, which means recognizing the comfort zone you have found yourself in and beginning to undermine the boundaries that keep that comfort zone intact. In a world where the tables of access to wealth, resources, and power are ever-shrinking, being a part of building a bigger table will provoke life as you extend the mercy of relationship beyond your comfort zone and receive that same mercy in return.

Jesus provides us with an example of a bigger table in the construction of His core group of followers - those whom He invested in the most. Within His crew were a tax collector and Zealot - one who collaborated with the Roman occupation and one bent on overthrowing it. There was one who would draw his sword to defend Jesus in the garden, and another whose betrayal led to his arrest there. And while not named as part of the original 12, there were most certainly women - those who would become the first witnesses of the resurrection. At the same time, history has forgotten several of their male counterparts.

Building a bigger table requires a shift in mindset. Jesus' answer to what it takes to inherit eternal life is simple: Love God and Love Neighbor. But who is your neighbor? The religious of Jesus' day wanted to know because their theology ascribed neighborly status to those closest to them and most like them. You probably define a neighbor the same way. Jesus blows that theology out of the water.

In the Parable of the Good Samaritan,[33] Jesus positions a people group hated by the religious elite as the hero of the story. He casts those whose religious devotion should compel them to help as those who pass by the beaten man without so much as a prayer. The hero, traveling on a dangerous road, takes on the burdens of one unknown to him and potentially unliked by him as his own. He doesn't just drop the man at the ER and continue on his way. The Samaritan not only secured the beaten man's safety but tended to his wounds and ensured the man would be provided for. Undoubtedly, they would have shared a meal, shared life, and built a relationship. The experience would forever link the two. When Jesus asked the religious leader inquiring about eternal life who in the story was the neighbor, it was the Samaritan who showed mercy.

The genius of Jesus in this parable is that He doesn't actually answer the question of who your neighbor is. He instructs on *how* to be a neighbor and uses one His culture would not usually see as a neighbor to define a neighbor as anyone God sends in your path. You have neighbors all around you, including those you prefer to avoid. If they are in your life, they are your neighbors and people God desires to show mercy to through you.

Because God's mercy is found in relationship with God and with others, those who call themselves Christians cannot be defined by our culture's rigidly promoted and enforced divisions, boundaries, and stratification. Otherwise, there will continue to be those outside who believe God is not for them. Where that is the case, Jesus went to the cross in vain.

Our willingness to show mercy by building a bigger table reflects our understanding of the mercy we have received. In another parable, Jesus tells of a man who owed an unfathomable amount of money. Justice in that culture would have called for the man and his family to be sold into slavery.[34] Out of compassion, and perhaps out of relationship, the master to whom the man was indebted forgives the debt and sets the debtor free.

However, faced with a similar opportunity over only a few pennies owed to him, the same man lords this debt over another and has this debtor thrown in jail. The master catches wind of this, reverses course on the original debt forgiveness, and has the man thrown in prison. Jesus told His listeners that this is what God will do to them and you and I when we don't show mercy in the way mercy has been shown to us.

This parable specifically references forgiveness, but the principle applies to the fullness of God's mercy. In mercy, God built a bigger table with room for you. In mercy, God sent Jesus to listen, care, and relate to and with you. In mercy, God has given you access through Christ to true, full, and authentic life. If you are unwilling to extend that same kind of mercy and, in doing so, provoke life outside your comfort zone, then you prove yourself to be an unworthy recipient of the mercy you have received, much like the man from Jesus' parable.

There are two ways to respond to this reality. The first is to react with fear that the grace you have promised your whole Christian life might be at risk, but then seek to theologize it away so that you still are in God's good graces but don't actually have to do anything different. This is not helpful and demonstrates that you don't understand that grace.

The other response is one grounded in gratitude for the mercy that you have received. Out of that gratitude flows the motivation to be part of building a bigger table, celebrating the diversity of all kinds in God's Kingdom and your community, and longing for the mercy of relationship with that diversity for yourself. This response will lead you to join Jesus in breaking down boundaries and subverting social stratification.

Some of my most meaningful ministry experiences came through trying to build a bigger table. In college, I served in a parachurch youth ministry whose primary strategy was to meet students on their turf and earn the right to be heard with the Gospel. Our best opportunity for this was to go to the school lunch room and hang out with students while they were eating.

At first, I spent most of my time with kids already involved in our ministry. They tended to be the popular, extroverted, and involved kids. But after a while, I began to look around and see a lunchroom full of students we were not engaging. I heard whispered accusations of favoritism, as though we as leaders only came to the school to see "the cool kids." And at our weekly gatherings, those we were accused of preferring were the only demographic present.

James, the brother of Jesus and the eventual leader of the early church in Jerusalem, had some harsh words to say about those who show favoritism. He writes in his letter, "You do well when you really fulfill the royal law found in scripture, *Love your neighbor as yourself*. But when you show favoritism, you are committing a sin, and by that same law you are exposed as a lawbreaker."[35]

The burden I felt was that of one guilty of not loving *all* the neighbors in my path - those students in the lunchroom who were in just as much need of God's love, grace, and mercy as the students to whom I had so easily gravitated. Repenting and seeking the forgiveness of God, I asked for my eyes and heart to be open to those most in need of the mercy of relationship, those for whom no seat at the table has been created. Jesus called me to build a bigger table in a high school lunchroom.

I wish I could tell stories of breakthroughs due to this shift in my ministry approach. Honestly, I have no idea what, if any, impact was made. It was hard work at first as I had to contend with their perceptions of me as one biased towards the popular crowd. I had to keep showing up until they eventually saw my desire for a relationship with them as genuine. And even then, my invitations to our ministry gatherings and programs were rebuffed.

While these young people found mercy coming from me, they remained unconvinced of what they would receive from others who were a part of the ministry, particularly their peers who benefited from the rigidly defined social strata of a high school and usually ignored them or worse.

This is why building a bigger table is a community or congregation's task, not just a lone individual's. Because of the reputation Christians have earned amongst those disconnected from church and faith, you and your faith community must be intentional in looking for who is missing amongst you. You must be gracious and sincere in your effort to build relationships and patient in earning the right to be heard. You must also be sensitive to the trauma so many carry around church and faith and not see them as objects for you to preach at.

Instead, you must view yourselves as conduits of mercy, not looking to solve their problems according to what you believe are the solutions, but first listening, caring, and relating to and with them.

These simple acts of relationship will demonstrate the mercy of God, and, along the way, you will be blessed by the relationships you build, even if you do not immediately see the Gospel impact of those relationships.

Even today, my now-wife sometimes needs to remind me that my job is not to solve what I think her problems are. Listening, caring, and relating to and with her have been critical disciplines in my role as her husband. When I see that as my end goal in our conversations, the mercy of relationship flows freely between us. She benefits from that mercy. So do I.

I would be remiss if I did not address the showing of mercy to a particular type of person to whom extending mercy is exceedingly difficult: those who have wounded us, wronged us, or even acted in abusive ways towards us.

How do you build a bigger table with space for those who have injured you? Does Jesus really intend of us to show them mercy? What does that look like?

(A trigger warning here for those who have experienced physical or sexual abuse. To avoid this content, skip the next section)

* * *

In the same sermon the Beatitudes appear, Jesus calls His disciples to show mercy even when they are treated unjustly.[36] But for those who have experienced any kind of abuse, these words can be difficult to swallow. They are words that have been weaponized against the victims of abuse, used by abusers to demand they remain in a toxic relationship. I've heard of abusive husbands striking their spouses, then demanding they "turn the other cheek" so that spouse could be struck again.

To be clear, the words of Jesus *do not* condone abuse of any kind, nor are they to be leveraged against the abused to remain vulnerable to the abuser. This a perverse twisting of the teaching of Jesus, who always stood on the side of the abused and vulnerable. While I believe there is grace available to all, I believe there is wrath for those who are unrepentant of the harm they create, and store up additional wrath when they use Scripture as justification.

And yet, the command of Jesus to show mercy remains and is intended for all people, regardless of the harm they have caused and may even continue to cause. In these situations, mercy may look very different and the space at Jesus' table for those who commit wrongs against others at that table may be subject to certain prerequisites.

An example of this is when a registered sex offender requests to join a local congregation. Of all expressions of human sinfulness, acts of sexual abuse are perhaps the most devastating in their impact. While these sins are not unforgivable before God, the reality of the perversion behind them means they cannot be forgotten before the world. To build a bigger table where there is space for those who have committed these acts, boundaries must be established and adhered to in order to ensure the inclusion of the (hopefully) reformed abuser and any previous or potential victims.

While Jesus' mercy leads us to build a bigger table, that doesn't mean that all people in all places have to make a bigger table for one individual. If someone has abused someone else in your congregation, for example, it becomes another congregation's job to create a space at the table for that person. Mercy is often something we provide as the entire Body of Christ. If you are unable to provide it for a specific individual, Jesus invites you to set your boundaries to let another community or individual do that work.

* * *

(Those avoiding the above content can safely resume reading here)

While they often don't feel like it to those who have wronged us, boundaries are mercy. They protect and provide a pathway for inclusion at Jesus' bigger table. And while it may be your responsibility to set those boundaries, it may not be your responsibility to go beyond that and help the person who has wronged you find a place. There are others in that person's life far better positioned than you to help them find space. At minimum, you are free in Christ to turn that responsibility over to God.

A prayer I would invite you to consider is one of the Lord's blessings over their life. In many relationships where there is conflict, trauma, and abuse, one may have a "blessing" or outcome in mind for what they want from the other party. The unfortunate reality is that these outcomes are often not realized.

But God has a blessing in mind, and so rather than remaining emotionally attached to the outcome of your desire, surrender that outcome to Jesus and seek in prayer for the blessing He has for you and for your situation. And perhaps, the blessing of the Lord may serve to transform the situation in ways you could have never imagined or manufactured yourself.

The mercy in this posture is not just for them. It is also for you. It has been said that holding out on extending mercy is like drinking a bottle of poison and expecting the other person to die. Whether it be through spiritual disciplines, therapeutic relationships, or restorative justice, even you can get to the place of being able to extend mercy to those who have wounded, wronged, or subjected you to abuse, the release of that burden through mercy will be mercy to you as well. You will more readily take your seat at Jesus' bigger table *and* more willingly help Him build it.

Demonstrating the mercy of God according to the Spirit's lead and, in doing so, revealing the Kingdom of God is not a means to an end. It is the end goal of a follower of Jesus and will provoke the true, full, authentic life Jesus came to bring.

APPLICATION

What you can do: Take a walk around your neighborhood. Notice the diversity present, and compare the households you spend time with and those you don't. Pick one neighbor who is different from you that you do not know very well and initiate a conversation. Pray for them and for opportunities to deepen a relationship through listening, caring, and relating to and with them.

What your church can do: Assess the barriers and divisions within your congregation. Whose needs and desires are at the center, and whose are marginalized? Does everyone have a seat at the table, or is favoritism being shown to some? Ensure the table is big enough for all and there is room for those beyond your walls.

Discussion Questions:

1. What is your response when someone shares a problem with you? Do you seek to solve it for them or take it as an opportunity to listen, care, and relate to and with them?
2. What do you think about Sunday being the most segregated hour of the week? Is that true in your congregation?
3. Who might you extend the mercy of relationship to that is outside your comfort zone? How might you encourage your faith community to join you in this?

Turn From The Counterfeit To Receive The Real

Blessed are the pure in heart, for they will see God.

Matthew 5:8

The closest thing I ever came to meeting a celebrity was when I rented a car to Jim J. Bullock. Jim J. is a comedian I watched on the Hollywood Squares game show as a kid. Nice guy. C-List celebrity at best.

I am not sure what I'd do if I saw a real celebrity out in the world. At first, I probably wouldn't believe my eyes. I'd probably move from disbelief to confusion over what they were doing in the same place I was. I'd likely shift to avoidance when I finished processing the confusion. After all, celebrities are real people with real priorities, and talking to me is not one of them. And what would I have to talk about?

I think this is a bit like how people feel when they hear phrases like "seeing God," "learning to hear from God for yourself," or "knowing God's will for your life." For many people, including Christians, the idea that God can be seen, heard, or known can feel a bit disorienting.

At first, you might not believe any of that is possible. Even if you think it is possible, you might be confused about how it happens. And perhaps you aren't all that sure you want it for yourself because once God is seen, heard, and known, whatever it is God wants from and for you becomes exponentially harder to ignore.

Our capitalistic reality means that many of us view our occupations as the chief place where our calling resides. Through my life, I went through a progression of career aspirations spanning from delusional (Major League Baseball player) to aspirational (prosecuting attorney). I even began my college career as a Pre-Law major. God hijacked those plans early in my college career with a profound revelation that my calling was to occupational ministry in some form or fashion. It was a calling I couldn't get away from, even if it took 18 years for that calling to be realized.

During those 18 years, even when I would have success through other vocations, first as a college student and campus leader, and then later in the business world, those successes never quite seemed to satisfy. Once I achieved the desired level of success somewhere, I quickly lost interest in continuing in that role. There was always this sense of something more meaningful out there, and so I kept looking for it.

I've heard that feeling called "holy discontent." It's not quite the same as ambition, which is the seeking of better for one's own sake. It's more about that whisper in your heart of a destiny beyond your current station. And while Scripture tells us to be content in all circumstances[37], that doesn't preclude you and I from discerning the source of our discontent and whether it is holy - as in a call to something different. I felt a calling to Christian public leadership.

To be clear, I am not glamorizing ministry. It is exceedingly taxing. There are plenty of other fields I could have pursued that would have provided greater financial security, less frustration, and a better "work/life balance." My last job was in banking, which offered all of those possibilities. It was a great job and I am grateful to have worked in that field. I was blessed by it in many ways, but towards the end, I was miserable. It was the counterfeit, and I was desperate for the real.

To call a career path or other life pursuit counterfeit is not to imply that it is bad. It simply doesn't align with the best version of who you are. Only the real can do that. It isn't a real calling if you are able to avoid it without feeling that impossible-to-ignore tug in a different direction. In the movie *The Matrix*, Morpheus called the awareness of the counterfeit "a splinter in your brain driving you mad." That's one way to define holy discontent.

There is nothing inherently wrong or bad about a life lived in pursuit of a secular career. It can *absolutely* be a calling to someone else and a place the Spirit sends you. In fact, I often tell people consider occupational ministry that if they can do *anything* else as a job and feel satisfaction in their life, they should do that other thing. For me, I couldn't because those other pursuits were counterfeit to who I was.

It took me 18 years to get here for several reasons. I think the Spirit's hand was definitely on the timing. There was maturation and formation that needed to take place. Occasionally, there would be a ministry opportunity that would present itself, but when I tried to pursue it, the door was closed quickly. The real does not always present itself right away, and until it does, the counterfeit can sustain you. Trusting God's timing is a part of "seeing God," "learning to hear from God for yourself," or "knowing God's will for your life."

That is true about more than just your career. God's calling on your life can be any place the Spirit sends you to die to yourself for the glory of God and for the service of someone else. Your calling might be to reside in a particular community, live out your faith in the context of your family, or stand with those who are oppressed and on the margins. You can also feel discontented about any pursuit in life. Discerning if that discontent is holy or not is, in and of itself, a holy act.

But what can also keep us from seeing, hearing, and knowing God is distraction. *The Office* is one of my favorite television shows ever, and in one episode, Michael Scott (the main character) wanders the city of

New York. He sees a woman he's sure is Tina Fey of Saturday Night Live fame. Michael approaches her for an autograph only to realize it isn't her at all. As he stares disappointed into the camera, late-night talk show host Conan O'Brien, a real celebrity, can be seen walking behind him. Michael was distracted by the counterfeit and missed the real.

You and I do this all the time. In pursuing our version of the good life, we chase after the counterfeit. We choose for ourselves a life that does not align with who we truly are because we don't know who we are. We follow that life as far as it can take us, only to find that it is not the true, full, and authentic life Jesus came to bring. All the while, Jesus is waiting to give us that life if only we would turn from the distraction of counterfeit living.

In Revelation 3, the risen Jesus dictates a letter to the church in Laodicea[38]. He accuses them of pursuing their version of the good life, a life of wealth, comfort, and security. They achieved The Laodicean Dream, which is not that different from The American Dream and our version of the good life. Jesus tells them that, despite their affluence, they are actually miserable, pathetic, poor, blind, and naked. Their poverty was spiritual. Again, not that different from the spiritual poverty of so many today, both inside and outside the Church.

But Jesus offers them a way out of that spiritual poverty. "Look! I'm standing at the door and knocking. If any hear my voice and open the door, I will come in to be with them, and will have dinner with them, and they will have dinner with me."[39] To share a meal with Jesus was to learn from Jesus the way to true, full, and authentic life, turning away from the counterfeit in favor of the real.

"Seeing God," "learning to hear from God for yourself," or "knowing God's will for your life" is your birthright as a child of God. But having a birthright and taking hold of a birthright are two different things. You are free in Christ to let go of the counterfeit version of the good life to take hold of the real version. When you do this, you see yourself clearly for the first time. You know who you are and what you are called to do. This is likely what Jesus meant when He said that those who are pure in heart would be blessed.

A few years ago, I surveyed my congregation members to learn more about their faith lives and the ways they wanted to grow. One of the questions I asked them was to name the aspect of their spirituality they most wanted to develop. Among possible answers like "worship," "serving," "generosity," and "Bible study" was "understanding God's will for my life." The latter was by far the most popular response.

I was surprised by the results because so many in my church have been Christians most of their lives. In follow-up conversations, it was clear that, for all their church involvement, there was a real lack of clarity in many about what God wanted them to do besides come to church. I was grateful that they desired to see, hear, know and understand God's will but saddened they had gone so long without developing that ability.

To say that God wants something from you can sound like God's grace is contingent on you measuring up to God's standard. This is a version of legalism that should be avoided. But God does want you to do something. The consistent witness of Scripture is that God has a will for you and me. Generally, we are to love God with the entirety of our being and to love others as much or more as we love ourselves. Vertical love toward God and horizontal love toward the world demand some action.

That action will be unique to you because you are unique. God has wired you with a personality, gifts, strengths, experiences, and perspectives. You will express love to God and others differently than I will based on that uniqueness. This is the beauty of the diversity of the Kingdom of God. It is God's will for you to be the best version of yourself, whatever that version might be. The key is to remember who decides what that best version is. It isn't defined by you or the world in which you live. It is defined by who you are in Christ. Living from that identity is God's version of the Good Life.

Aligning your life to God's will does not earn you God's grace. It is *because* of God's grace that you align yourself to God's will. You will love God and love others and express that love in action because of the grace you have received. When you express vertical and horizontal love, you will see God at work in you and through you into the lives of others. You will provoke life.

What often keeps you from "seeing God," "learning to hear from God for yourself," or "knowing God's will for your life" are the various distractions you and I face daily. Perhaps you've been told by the world there is a version of life you are to pursue and that your thriving depends on achieving that life. It might lead you to take that pressure on yourself, dividing your attention between God's will for your life and the achievement of the life you've become convinced you need.

Over time, the distractions causing that division overtake your attention, and there is no longer room for seeing, hearing, and knowing God. The closest you come to understanding God's will for your life is making the best decision you can based on your understanding and hoping God will bless it. More often than not, however, is that there is little awareness of what God is doing in your life. What was to be your birthright can become a vague afterthought.

This Beatitude promises that the pure in heart will see God, an idea that would have caused as much anxiety as it would anticipation in Jesus' listeners. Throughout the Old Testament, people would hide their faces from the presence of God, aware of their sinfulness. They held onto the hope that one day, they would achieve the necessary purity to, as David wrote in Psalm 24, ascend the Lord's mountain and stand in the holy sanctuary. But how they defined purity and the purity that Jesus is after aren't the same.

When Jesus spoke of purity of heart as the way to see God, He didn't mean moral or ritual purity. God does not only reveal Himself to those with good behavior. Purity of heart refers to singleness of motive and focus. Rather than having a mind divided by the demands of job, family, school, money, and the other concerns of this life, Jesus calls you to have one singular focus. Your call is to provoke life and help Him change the world through the expression of vertical and horizontal love in whatever role you play at the moment.

Imagine your life as though it were a chest of drawers, where each role you play and concern you carry has its own drawer. You might have a drawer dedicated to your job or your education. If you are married or have kids, there might be a drawer for each. Your finances would have their own drawer, and given how much our culture is tied up in pursuing and managing wealth, it would probably be a big drawer. Your relationships, hobbies, health, and every other aspect of your life would be arranged as drawers on this chest also.

The mistake a lot of Christians make is assigning Jesus a drawer alongside the rest. The Jesus drawer is perhaps opened only on Sunday, when you are going through a difficult time, or facing a difficult decision. Once you have gotten what you need from that drawer, you close it up until the next time you need something from it or when religion demands you open it once more.

"Compartmentalized Christianity" is common in our culture, but it is not a helpful way of thinking about the role of Jesus in your life. Don't feel guilty if this is where you are because everyone is battling this to some degree. But it is the likely cause for your difficulty in seeing, hearing, knowing, and understanding God's will for your life.

Jesus is not a drawer. He is the whole chest within which everything else finds its place. Your identity in Christ can bring clarity to every other role you play. Adopting this understanding is the path to a pure heart and a mind not divided by the distractions and demands of your life. You will have genuine clarity about God's will because you have placed the entirety of your life in God's hands.

So much of what drives a divided mind and lack of focus on God's will is an emotional attachment to a particular outcome. That attachment drives a discontent that is *not* holy. Purifying your heart with a focus on understanding God's will for your life begins when you detach emotionally from the outcomes you want for yourself and become open to wherever the Spirit will lead you. Simply put, it means you no longer value a different version of life - a counterfeit version - than the one God longs for you to have, which is the real.

When I was in seminary, I also worked for the ELCA, running a college ministry in my hometown. I loved it and thought it was my long-term calling, even beyond seminary graduation and ordination. What stood in the way was a required year-long internship that would take me away from my college ministry role.

In the year before my internship, I implored my denominational officials to let me stay in my role for the internship. I felt that everything I needed to experience could happen where I was. Why did I need to uproot my family and ministry from the community we built? I was emotionally attached to the outcome of what I wanted for my life, and I kept running into brick walls to make it happen.

There is a song performed by Michael W. Smith with the lyric, "You are working in our waiting/You're sanctifying us/When beyond our understanding/You're teaching us to trust."[40] I first heard this song in a worship service six months before my internship was scheduled to begin. My efforts to dictate this experience's terms prevented a suitable site from being identified. I was concerned both for the ministry I would have to prepare for my leaving and my progress towards ordination, which could be delayed if I could not find an internship site.

I went to a worship service that morning with the heaviness of my situation more pronounced than usual. When the lyrics popped on the screen, it was like someone had knocked the wind out of me. In my season of frustration, it had felt as though God was silent and I was alone, hurtling toward my future with no sense of security. That morning, I was reminded that God is always working, especially when I was waiting. While I did not understand why, I needed to trust the Spirit's work in the process and let go of my emotional attachment to my future in ministry.

When I got home, I contacted one of the denominational staff I was working with to let her know I was open to whatever internship experience they could find and that I would trust the Spirit's leading. A short time later, an internship site emerged that met all the criteria my denomination was looking for and prepared me for ordained ministry in ways my college ministry role never could have.

Detaching emotionally from the outcome I wanted and surrendering to what God wanted for me took me on a path towards ordination I could not have imagined for myself, and I am grateful. As good as my version of the internship seemed to me, it was the counterfeit. What God provided was the real.

Much of my attachment to a preferred outcome was rooted in a lack of trust that the path unfolding before me would be the best. I felt I needed to figure out my way and arrange for it, or else I would not be ok. As much as I professed to trust in Jesus, this attachment to my preferred outcome revealed a lack of trust that hindered me from seeing God at work in the process.

Turning away from compartmentalized Christianity towards understanding that your whole life flows from, with, and in Jesus will reveal the true nature of your discontent. Sometimes, what we want flows out of temptation for that which God has not promised. Sometimes, our discontent is because what God has promised has not happened yet. And, there are even sometimes when God's timing is not what is delaying God's promise, but instead, the promise is being delayed by systemic injustices outside of our control.

Regardless, the answer is to press into your relationship with Jesus, both as an individual disciple and in the context of community.

Jesus extends a promise to His disciples and to us that God will care for us. He points to the provision given to the birds of the air and the flowers of the field. They always have what they need, and God loves you far more than those. When you seek first God's Kingdom with a pure heart, you will start "seeing God," "learning to hear from God for yourself," and "knowing God's will for your life."[41]

You might be tempted to look around at our world and see all the people who don't have enough, for whom life does not seem to work out, and who lack direction. You may even consider yourself as this kind of person. This certainly can undermine the trust Jesus is calling you and me to here.

Remember Jesus' audience. Jesus taught and led people from the lowest socioeconomic class, who routinely did not have enough, for whom life was not working, and who were so lacking in direction that the Bible called them "sheep without a shepherd." If His promise to them was one of provision and direction, you can be assured that promise extends to you.

As someone who is often frustrated by what appears to be God's slowness, I know how difficult this can be, especially when what I am waiting on God to do feels like life or death. Because you and I lack the eternal and omniscient perspective of God, we can quickly descend into despair when we do not receive that which we believe God has promised us.

To what are you emotionally attached? Are those attachments grounded in Jesus' version of life for you? Or do those attachments fall outside what you've entrusted to Jesus? Suppose you are stressed out and running into proverbial brick walls in your attempts to progress according to those attachments. In that case, you could be emotionally attached to something Jesus never promised you. If you want to see, hear, know, and understand God's will for your life, detach emotionally and turn from the counterfeit to receive the real.

Your pursuit of the counterfeit, a version of the good life different from God's, does not happen by accident. Every one of us wants to be God over our lives, dictate the terms of our pursuits, and define what our lives should and will become. We believe we are the ones responsible for ordering and filling the chest of drawers that make up our lives.

When you join Jesus in His death by allowing Him to put your version of the good life to death, it will provoke the true, full, and authentic version of life Jesus brought. You are no longer responsible for ordering and filling the chest of drawers, which was too much of a burden for you to handle. The pressure and stress of having to create that life have kept you from seeing, hearing, knowing, and understanding God's will for your life, but no more.

As you turn from the counterfeit to receive the real, Jesus will cut through the distraction and replace disbelief, confusion, and avoidance with His grace, which creates within you a pure heart and desire for others to see, hear, know, and understand God's will for their lives, as well. The life that is provoked within you will overflow and will begin to help Jesus change the world around you. As you see God more clearly and respond in faith to what you see, those around you will see God in you as you become more and more like the Jesus you follow. You will provoke life simply because you are living out the character of Jesus.

APPLICATION

What you can do: Your inability to see, hear, know, and understand God's will for your life could be grounded in the compartmentalization of your faith. If Jesus is just one drawer in your life, you will only hear from him when that drawer is opened. So begin to shift how you understand Jesus's role in your life. On a piece of paper, list every role you play in the world, your most important relationships, and how you spend your time. At the top of the page, write JESUS in big letters. Then, each day, pick one aspect and reflect on how Jesus might want to work in and through you in that role, relationship, or activity.

What your church can do: Learning to see, hear, know, and understand God's will in the context of community can go a long way in helping people get past disbelief, confusion, and avoidance of the presence of God at work in their lives. Our congregation asks people each week in worship to share "God Sightings," which I define as blessings, positive events, or things they have learned about God or themselves. Getting people talking together about God being active and moving serves as an encouragement to set aside distractions and look for God daily. What might a similar practice look like in your church?

Discussion Questions:

1. Have you ever run into a celebrity in real life? How did you feel when you saw them? What did you do?
2. What goes through your head when you hear or read the phrases "seeing God," "learning to hear from God for yourself," or "knowing God's will for your life?"
3. What counterfeit versions of life have you chosen that Jesus calls you to turn from?

Wage Peace By Wearing Love

Blessed are the peacemakers, for they will be called children of God.

Matthew 5:9

As kids grow up, eventually, the family to which they are born begins to carry a particular identity or reputation. It may be a cause the family organizes around, an activity they regularly participate in together, or an organizing principle they seek to live by. In unfortunate cases, some families are known for their dysfunctions. Intentionally or not, your family was or is known by those you're in relationship with for something.

As a pastor, the most natural identity my family has picked up is through our involvement with our church. Not only do I lead the church, but my wife is also on staff part-time, and my kids spend a significant amount of time in the building. They have held birthday parties at the church, taken music lessons in the church, and even invited friends to the church building for play dates. We are blessed that our church is not only a place they *have* to spend time in but a place they *want* to be. I hope they won't embody many of the negative stereotypes surrounding PKs (pastor's kids) as they get older.

God's family has a cause, an activity, and an organizing principle, or at least it should. If you and I are God's children and embody what

God's family should be about, then those beyond the walls of the Church should see Christians as peacemakers, since, in this Beatitude, that is who Jesus said will be called God's children.

Peace is hard to come by in a world rife with division. On the international level, our world is dealing with war in Ukraine, the ongoing conflict between Israel and the Palestinians, political unrest in Lebanon and Iraq, civil war in Myanmar, and a near failed state in Afghanistan. There are currently 27 ongoing conflicts worldwide at the time of this writing. These conflicts affect billions of lives, creating humanitarian crises, economic catastrophes, and rampant injustice.

Here in America, political, racial, and socioeconomic divisions continue to deepen. Studies show an increase in violence, the willingness to use violence to advance a partisan objective, and even a growing expectation of another civil war here in this country. The riot at the U.S. Capitol Building on January 6th, 2021 was a massive inflection point for this country. A line was crossed that was once thought uncrossable, fueled by cults of personality and rampant conspiracy theories. These forces don't seem to be going away. Unfortunately, some of their support comes from those who claim a Christian identity.

There has long been a belief that America is a "Christian" nation. While we enjoy religious freedom, and many of our citizens identify as Christian, much of what goes on in our country fails to reflect the message of Christ.

Lutheran theology gives us the term "Simul Justus et Peccator" which refers to humans as being sinners and saints simultaneously. It's this duel nature that explains why we are so quick to, as Brennan Manning put it, profess God with our lips and deny God with our lifestyle. America is the national embodiment of Simul Justes et Peccator.

For those who love America, it is difficult to look in the mirror and be honest about America. But being honest about where we are as a country is the only way for us to become what God calls us to be. We are the country that props up ruthless dictators in the name of freedom. We are the country that welcomes the poor, huddled masses as long as we like the country they came from. We are the country that feeds the world while drone-bombing civilians. We are the country that wants so desperately to believe in our inherent goodness that we are blind to our inherent sinfulness. We are the country that considers itself a Christian nation and yet looks very little like the Kingdom Jesus brought.

Compare what you see running rampant in America with the prophet Isaiah's description of a nation seeking after the heart of God[42], who will:

- Walk in God's paths
- Submit to God to settle disputes
- Beating weapons into tools for fruitfulness
- Renouncing war against other nations

If that is what it means to be a "Christian" nation, America (and every other country in the world, for that matter) is far from becoming what God intended for us. To be clear, I am not saying America should try to be a Christian nation - in fact, I don't think that should be a goal. It certainly was not a goal of our nation's founders, nor do I think Jesus wants that for us.

Jesus was never particularly concerned with earthly nations or kingdoms. He did not advocate for specific policy positions or the elevation of a particular governmental official. His concern was that justice was being done by the religious and political systems of His day, who had combined to govern the people. He decried the religious leaders' co-opting of God's Law for their own power, and He refused to bow down to the Roman overlords when brought face-to-face with Pilate.

If Jesus believed the existing power structures of His day and ours could make peace, He would have focused His attention on winning over those in power to His cause. Instead, He promised citizenship in a Kingdom that was not of this world and adoption into a family that would be known by their love for God and one another by those without power. Contrary to the nations of the world who sought to wage war, the "nation" Jesus established would wage peace by wearing love.

Love is often framed as an emotion you feel for another person, but Scripture frames love as an intentional choice, like a wardrobe you choose to put on. The Apostle Paul writes that you and I are to "put on love, which is the perfect bond of unity."[43] Unity can only exist where peace has been made, and you can only commit to making peace with others when you have received the peace of God. This peace "must control your hearts—a peace into which you were called in one body."[44]

The reason for division, whether at the international, national, or even household level boils down to not feeling secure in a relationship. Unfortunately, that insecurity can lead to destructive and unnecessary actions. Russia doesn't feel secure with NATO expansion and the actions of the Ukrainian government, so it attacks. Members of one political party feel threatened by the policy objectives of the other, so they start slinging mud. A spouse does not feel their partner has their best interests at heart and believes they must fight for their needs to be met.

While conflict in human relationships is unavoidable, you and I were not meant to live divided from one another. We are far better off leaning into what unites us than drawing the lines that divide us.

We are reconciled to God in Christ, but Jesus does not stop there. He is intent on seeing you and I reconciled to one another and find security in our relationships with God and one another. Humanity has erected physical, social, and financial barriers to keep humans apart in the name of security. Jesus has every barrier that separates one human from another in His sights. As beings created in the image of a God that exists in the community of the Trinity, you and I cannot reflect that image without being in community with one another. The peace of God must be present between us for the bonds of a loving relationship to be securely forged.

The peace of God provokes life, but peace will not just happen on its own. Peace has to be made; therefore, you and I must be makers of that peace. You and I must wage peace, and we wage peace by wearing love, putting it on as though it were an article of clothing that communicated something about who we are. It's like the athlete whose high school awards her a "letter" to fix to a jacket. Walking down the hall with such a jacket would proclaim something about the person's identity. It would bind the athlete with peers who have achieved similarly. And, on some level, it would inspire others to similar achievements.

This is why Jesus did not look to the systems of power in His day to achieve His objectives. If He wanted His Kingdom to come through those means, He would have allowed the people following Him to lead a revolution and make Him king by force, as they wanted to in John 6. He would not have told Peter to put his sword away in the garden. He would not have submitted to death on the cross. True peace cannot be made unless it is grounded in love, and love cannot be instituted through power, force, and might. It must be "put on."

Waging peace by wearing love begins with joining Jesus in His death and being raised to a new and different kind of life. While you do not physically die as Jesus did for this to happen, you must give up your right to be right. The hurdles to peace are often built on offense, a desire to regain lost power or control, or the impulse for revenge. Reprisal is so often the precursor for the collapse of peace. The death of pride and ego is required for this response, whether that be at the individual or national level.

It may sound naive to advocate for waging peace in this manner, but ask yourself a question. Is our system of revenge and reprisal in response to being wronged working? Is it working for us to remain isolated from and suspicious of one another? Does this way of being forge lasting peace and loving relationships? Or is there a better way - one where desiring to remain in relationship where possible is placed at a far higher value than being right or achieving revenge?

The story of Abram and Lot is an excellent example of this better way. Abram received God's promise of becoming a great nation, and yet, when he and Lot arrived in the land God was planning to give them, they found that it was not big enough for the both of them. There were too many livestock to feed, possessions to store, and servants to manage. Conflict broke out between the two families.

While Abram could have demanded his right to be right, he saw remaining in relationship as a far more important value. He offered Lot the opportunity to select first the property Lot would dwell on, knowing his nephew would choose the most fertile land with the best potential for abundance. This would have relegated Abram to living amongst those who would become sworn enemies of God's people. Abram did this willingly, even enthusiastically, because he trusted in God's promise. This security freed Abram to wage peace by wearing his love for his nephew through sacrifice.

This is the same self-sacrificing love that led Jesus to take up His cross willingly. It is the self-sacrificing love that will lead you to take up your cross, denying yourself and following Him. Self-sacrificing love is the only sustainable path to peace. Waging peace means sometimes putting yourself or your own interests at risk. You can wear this love because your security is not found in the life you can arrange for yourself but in the security you have in the promises of God.

Waging peace by wearing love in your household might be subordinating your career interests for your spouse's benefit. I heard of a man who divorced his wife when she told him she would be unwilling to give up her job to move to wherever his next promotion in his company would send him. In a culture that expects women to put their careers on hold for the sake of their families, wearing love might have led him to pump the brakes on his ambitions and allow his wife's career to flourish after their daughter was born. It would have saved them a lot of heartbreak and kept their family intact.

Waging peace by wearing love in our national discourse might mean setting aside the pursuit of power and seeking to find common ground with those who oppose you, even if they advocate policies you vehemently disagree with. The political parties in our country seem far more interested in winning than they do governing. They entice us with the promise that if we give them the power they crave, we will get the country we want in the way we want it. It has never happened and will never happen. What has moved us forward as a nation is the willingness to listen, understand, and work together to forge a compromise everyone can live with, even if we don't get everything we want.

Waging peace by wearing love internationally might mean ceasing our national interests as the primary driver of our global engagement. "America First" is galvanizing rhetoric, but it does not align with the Gospel of Jesus Christ. Instead, we should be looking to partner with others to promote the flourishing of all nations, not just ours and our allies. I do not claim to be a foreign policy expert, but I am not sure the world has ever seen this kind of engagement. I wonder how much better off our world would be if we could all find a way to remove the blinders of nationalism and realize the only real differences between us are some lines on a map.

No matter where in the world you live or what culture you have been formed by, most human beings ultimately want the same things. We want to feel security and stability. We want to have enough to meet our needs. We want assistance when we stumble or struggle. We want our families and our children (if we have them) to thrive. Waging peace by wearing love embraces the unifying nature of these wants and seeks to ensure all can have these desires met, even if it means you are making sacrifices.

While the call of Christ is to wage peace by wearing love, peacemaking does not always lead to peace-achieving. You must also find "partners in peace." Your spouse may not place your interests ahead of theirs as you place theirs ahead of yours. Those who disagree with you may be unwilling to meet you at a table of listening, understanding, and compromising. Some nations will never truly seek peace because their leaders greatly value power and control. How do you make peace amongst those for whom peace is not a priority?

Jesus' words in Matthew 18 have been used in both helpful and unhelpful ways for "church discipline," but these words also provide a framework for peacemaking without a partner. When there is a conflict, you begin by seeking to make peace directly with the person with whom you have conflict. If that does not work, you introduce neutral third parties to assist in mediating. If peace can still not be achieved, you bring the conflict to a broader assembly. After exhausting these avenues without a breakthrough of peace, you release them from your relationship but remain open to the possibility of restoration down the road.

What Jesus laid out was intended to be a restorative process in which peace could be waged as the two parties intentionally put on their love for God and one another. While it is true that you cannot always expect those outside of the Church to engage in a process like this (although some may), you should be able to expect from your siblings within the Body of Christ. And they should be able to expect it from you. Unfortunately, more often than not, rather than deal with the conflicts between us as individuals, we find it easier to cut ourselves off from those we feel have wronged us. Ghosting allows us to avoid difficult conversations but robs us of the potential for reconciliation and robs others of the opportunity to make it right.

As a pastor, I have made mistakes, hurt people, or failed to live up to their expectations. Others have done the same to me. Unfortunately, in most cases, I have never been allowed the opportunity to restore the relationship, despite repeated attempts at trying. In the rare times where I have been able to sit with someone who has wronged me or who I have wronged, we have been able to reconcile, forgive, and forge a new and often stronger relationship. The pain of the conflict has been overshadowed by the joy of peace being made.

Waging peace by wearing love should not be confused with conflict avoidance, turning a blind eye to injustice, or ignoring abuse. Sometimes, waging peace means speaking the truth others would rather not hear. When there are power dynamics involved, speaking truth to power may be the only way to wear love for those being oppressed by that power. And sometimes, those impacted by the lack of peace do not possess the strength and stability to wage peace for themselves. The responsibility falls to those who do to wage peace on their behalf. This, too, is putting on love.

My denomination recently experienced a version of this. While many of our ecclesiastical leaders are fine people with good intentions, the system is structured in such a way that, when abuses take place against vulnerable stakeholders, it is *really* difficult for justice to be achieved and peace to be made. In one of our regional expressions, called synods, a dispute arose regarding the handling of abuse allegations against a Latinx pastor.

While the pastor proclaimed his innocence, called for an open investigation and due process, and sought reconciliation, the bishop of that synod took punitive actions that appeared to have exceeded what was necessary and appropriate for the handling of this case. This led to the removal of the pastor from the primarily Latinx congregation he had started and the disruption of worship of that community, beginning on one of its most holy celebrations and continuing to this very day. Because of how our system is structured and particularities of that pastor's role, he had no official means of recourse. He was simply removed from the clergy roster without a chance to appeal.

As word got out, there were some who called for all parties to trust the process and wait for the truth to come out. Those in executive leadership positions in the national office attempted to claim they had no authority to step in. But as more of the facts of the case came to light, it became clear that an injustice was done against this pastor and the people he served. Voices across the denomination rose to apply pressure on our leadership to act.

Eventually, the bishop of that synod, whose handling of the original allegations had created so much havoc, resigned and those allegations are now being adjudicated in a more peace-making and transparent way. This would not have been possible if those with the privilege to speak without the risk of reprisal had not done so. While I am sure some who spoke out did so out of anger and a desire for revenge, there were many who were motivated by a love for the Church and for the people involved. It does not diminish the tragedy of the circumstances, nor the fact that there are still allegations against the pastor that need to be resolved. Uncertainty still remains as the process of truth-seeking continues. But it serves as an example using one's voice on behalf of the vulnerable and the power of wearing love in an attempt to wage peace.

It is tempting to get caught up in the way of the world that leads to division. Scarcity and fear can draw you into arranging for your life according to your interests without regard for the interests of others. The right to be right is powerful and attractive. Others might find it foolish to do otherwise, but, as a follower of Jesus, the wisdom of this world does not govern you. The wisdom of Christ, in which self-sacrificing love is the primary value, rules your life. You might even suffer unjustly as a result. But suffering unjustly in the pursuit of peacemaking is a powerful witness.

Think about the changes to our world wrought by civil disobedience and nonviolent resistance compared to the aftermath of riots. Reflect on the marriage disputes resolved through counseling and mediation compared to scorched-earth divorce proceedings. While the long game of diplomacy is slow and frustrating, compare it to the tragedy of war and the havoc it causes.

As Gandhi is purported to have said, "An eye for an eye leaves the whole world blind." Life is not provoked through participation in division. Jesus wants to change the world through peacemaking, and He wants your help. It is the call of Christ on every disciple of Jesus to put down your right to be right, to put on love, and to wage peace. This calling is a sign of your identity as a child of God. It is what God's family does.

APPLICATION

What you can do: Who in your life has wronged you? Who have you wronged? Reflect on the state of those relationships. To what degree have they been restored? Invite those you are not reconciled with into a Matthew 18 process grounded in your love for God and that person, if it is safe for you to do so.

What your church can do: Assess the fault lines of division in your community. Are there divisions along race, socio-economics, partisan politics, or other factors? Rather than stand apart from the division or pretend it doesn't exist, find ways to lovingly step into the division and lead your community towards peace. Not everyone will want to go with you, and there will be some who do not appreciate your presence, but this act of waging peace by wearing love will provoke life.

Discussion Questions:

1. Growing up, what was your family known for?

2. What are some ways America can be more Christ-like as a nation?
3. How might you be contributing to the divisiveness in our culture? What do you need to change in your life so that you will wage peace by wearing love?

Embrace the Danger of Difference

Blessed are those who are persecuted for the sake of righteousness, for theirs is the kingdom of heaven.

Matthew 5:10

In high school, I existed somewhere in the middle ground between the popular and the persecuted, at least in terms of how persecution manifests in an American suburban public school. I had friends, participated in school activities, and was mainly well-liked by other students across the "popularity" spectrum. I was also the subject of teasing on rare occasions and once had to dispatch a peer who was attempting to bully me with a right cross to his jaw. While the "in crowd" never invited me to parties, my high school experience was relatively persecution-free.

Some of my classmates couldn't say the same. I remember those who were mistreated and bullied, usually for differences outside their control. The economically-disadvantaged kids, those who spoke with impediments or were awkwardly shy, or those who were "different" in ways no one could put a finger on but everyone noticed received poor treatment. Bullying has always been a scourge on our schools, a problem that has only become more pervasive over time. Now, as a parent of elementary-aged kids, I am continually listening to their stories for signs that they might be victims of such treatment.

Whether you were bullied, a bully yourself, or someone like me, bullying is as close to persecution as many of us have experienced. You and I are blessed to live in a country that is tolerant of religious expression. Most forms of religious persecution are outlawed. You will probably not be killed, thrown in jail, evicted from your home, or separated from your family because you are a Christian. This is a privilege Christians in other parts of the world do not share. According to Open Doors, an international NGO advocating on behalf of persecuted Christians, "Across 76 countries, more than 360 million Christians suffer high levels of persecution and discrimination for their faith – an increase of 20 million since last year."[45]

While the United States is not one of those 76 countries, that does not prevent some American Christians from claiming persecution. Loss of privilege is often mistaken for persecution. Marriage equality, abortion access, and restriction on faith expression in schools are not evidence of persecution but necessary realities of the diverse and pluralistic society in which we live. For much of the 20th Century, Christianity held privileged status in our country, and as the late Ruth Bader Ginsburg said, "For those accustomed to privilege, equality feels like oppression."

Claiming persecution where none exists diminishes the experiences of those actually experiencing persecution. Having your beliefs questioned or challenged, experiencing discomfort in a changing world, or losing privileges you were never entitled to is not persecution.

That is not to say that no American Christian experiences persecution. When you face abuse, mistreatment, or hostility because you live according to the words, works, and ways of Jesus, that is persecution. An argument could be made that those guided by a Gospel of liberation who have been arrested, tear-gassed, or beaten for demonstrating against racial inequality, police brutality, and the rights of the otherwise marginalized in the name of Christ are victims of persecution.[46]

As one with colleagues who have lived these experiences, I can attest that it was their faith in Jesus and not some political agenda that led to lawful and peaceful demonstration, and yet they were the victims of violence because of their faith. Despite the characterizations by certain political and religious leaders regarding the motivations of those who stand for justice, what these colleagues and those who like them embraced was not a partisan ideology but faithful response to an evil they could no longer tolerate.

There is also a way in which those who live differently for the sake of Christ experience "systemic persecution." This persecution isn't wrought upon you by direct action from any one individual. Instead, as the direction of your life diverts from the priorities the rest of the world possesses as you follow Jesus, you will experience difficulties and miss out on opportunities because of that choice. The danger of difference won't manifest in threats to your life or livelihood but in diminishing access to what the world deems most valuable.

For example, I heard of a family who prioritized Sabbath rest. Every week on Sunday, they would attend worship, nap in the afternoon, and have friends and family over for dinner. The parents did not pursue any work for their jobs or household upkeep tasks, and the children did not participate in any extracurricular activities. Sunday was a day to engage with God, one another, and the broader community for rest and renewal. This was in keeping with the fourth commandment and the overarching Biblical mandate to steward your family well.

Setting aside one day a week in this manner may not seem like a costly decision, but saying yes to Sabbath meant saying no to several other priorities. Youth sports are particularly active on the weekends, and a determination to practice Sabbath would limit the advancement opportunities in athletics for the children. Not taking the weekend to attend to job responsibilities might mean less productivity in the eyes of a boss and create the appearance of being less committed to the company and less worthy of promotion.

These implications would have financial costs, perhaps in terms of scholarship opportunities for the kids and salary increases for the adults. Eventually, children or adults would experience the fear of missing out or the pain of being left behind. While that is not persecution in the way experienced by the early church, the global church, or those advocating on the margins, it is a danger of difference to which you and I can relate. First-world problems are still problems that seek to keep us from following Jesus.

The point here is not to encourage Sabbath keeping in this way for every household, as that is a practice made impossible for some due to financial inequalities, family dynamics, and living situations. There are any number of ways in which your household can construct a life that runs contrary to the prevailing paradigms of the world. Instead, the point is that this household felt led by the Spirit to embrace a spiritual practice that would set them at odds with the culture surrounding them. This choice would have a cost, but they embraced it because the benefits far outweighed that cost.

Life would be so much easier if you would just go with the flow of the world, or at least so you might think. And yet, the outcomes of embracing sameness with the do-more, work-harder, get-better, or else culture in which you and I live are destructive to our souls. There is a danger in following Jesus and being different, but going with the flow is far more dangerous. If you want the true, full, and authentic life Jesus promised, and if you're going to provoke that life in the world around us, you have to embrace the danger of difference.

What causes a disciple of Jesus to embrace the danger of difference? The prophet Jeremiah is an Old Testament hero who not only lived differently but called others to change and join him in that difference. Unfortunately, far too many in our world are comfortable with the status quo. Instead of rising to the challenge, they take out their frustration over the discomfort of change on the ones who call for that change. This was the experience of Jeremiah, and yet he lived differently anyway.

Dr. Henry Cloud, a respected Christian author, clinical psychologist, and leadership expert, speaks of three types of responses to challenge. The wise response is to bend yourself to the challenge and embrace it. The foolish response is to lean away from the challenge and reject it. The evil response is to not only reject the challenge but to "shoot the messenger." Even though it was in the people's best interest to embody wisdom, they responded to Jeremiah's prophetic challenge with foolishness and evil.

In Jeremiah 7, the prophet cries out to God, wanting badly to be released from the call to bring challenge and live differently. This call had cost Jeremiah dearly, and was threatening to cost him his life. But God had shown Jeremiah the destruction a failure to change would bring to God's people, and Jeremiah's love for God and his community sparked a fire in his heart that compelled him to speak. Jeremiah expressed trust that while he was subject to persecution, the Lord would be his defender, and those who opposed Jeremiah would ultimately fail.

This fire sparked by a love for God and community is what compels disciples of Jesus to embrace the danger of difference. You cannot manufacture it, nor can it be sustained by legalistic "shoulds." It is the faithful response to both the invitation of Jesus to receive His grace and the challenge to extend His grace to those with whom you would not otherwise interact. As the Apostle John wrote, "We love because God first loved us."[47] You will live differently because of the Spirit's work within you.

The unfortunate reality of this work and the difference you will embrace as a result is that it will expose you to danger. The further you go on your journey with Jesus, the more potentially dangerous it becomes. While there are varying degrees of danger in following Jesus depends on the context in which you operate, the danger is very real.

Jesus wants your help to change the world, but many do not want the world to change and will respond to you with foolishness or evil.

And yet, God is present with you in the danger of difference. In Psalm 31, David cries out to God much as Jeremiah did. David's soul was downcast due to the toll of suffering and harassment at the hands of those who opposed Him. Violence was plotted against him, and this distressed him greatly. But along with distress was an equal and opposite feeling: determination. David was determined to hold tightly to his faith in the deliverance that God had promised Him. David believed his future was in God's hands and that those who repaid his difference with danger would answer to God.

David could say this because of how God had worked in his life up to that point. In his panic over previous persecution, he felt cut off from God. But when David cried out to God, God heard his cries and demonstrated God's faithful love. This was a consistent theme in David's life, and he uses it to encourage his community and ours.

God sees your distress when you feel in danger from first-world problems of revoked opportunities or more severe threats of violence because of your faith. You can both fear harassment and suffering while trusting the Lord to protect and deliver you.

What helped David and can help you deal with the danger of difference is reflecting on how God has shown up for you in the past. When did you face struggle or suffering, either from persecution or some other cause? How did God show up for you?

I find that many Christians struggle to articulate the presence of God amid suffering and struggle. They shy away from potential danger because, deep down, they expect to go through it alone and without direction. The cost of embracing the danger of difference seems significant, and they lack the trust in God David displayed when he wrote, "All you who wait for the Lord, be strong and let your heart take courage."[48] And yet, when they are invited to consider all of the ways Jesus showed up for them in the past, they find those ways to be abundant.

The ways Jesus works in our lives can feel mysterious, but they are not a mystery. Perhaps God showed up for you through the comfort of a loved one. Perhaps God answered a prayer in a way that you could not have expected. Perhaps your struggle or suffering has not ended, but there is a peace that rules your heart that could only come from the Spirit. Perhaps you did not know it at the time, but God was using your suffering to prepare you for the next phase of your journey or so that you could bear witness to God's goodness on the other side.

As you reflect on the events of your life, particularly the moments where there was suffering and struggle, the Spirit may begin to illuminate for you how God had your back. This awareness can create the faith to believe that if you embrace the danger of difference, the Lord will guide you through whatever form of persecution comes your way.

And here is the uncomfortable truth: the danger of difference may be visited upon you before you are ready to embrace it. Peter writes in his first letter that you and I should not be surprised when "fiery trials" come[49]. Yet, how often do these trials come as a surprise? Your life plan might unfold in a blessed and joyful way until, seemingly out of nowhere, a conflict, circumstance, or choice confronts you and puts your commitment to your faith to the test. Will you continue on the path Jesus called you to, or will you take the road most traveled, the road that aligns with worldly priorities?

We've compromised ourselves by taking the easy way out, choosing the expedient or the extravagant over the eternal, and those choices have had consequences. At times, we have been the architects of our own struggle or suffering and, at times, been the architects of suffering and struggle for others. It is critical to acknowledge this truth as it will send us to Jesus, who sits on a throne of grace. He not only forgives us but empowers us to make different choices and promises to be with us when the danger of that difference emerges.

This does not mean you will not suffer. The early church suffered greatly for their faith in Christ and for embracing the danger of difference. While we live in a world with many examples of meaningless suffering, suffering for your faith is never meaningless. Frequently, God baptizes the danger of difference into a greater purpose.

The aftermath of the stoning of Stephen in Acts 8 is one example. Stephen was one of the first deacons in the early church, a key leader and gifted servant, but was stoned to death at the behest of the not-yet-converted Saul of Tarsus. Following this, the church faced extreme persecution. Most of the Christian community in Jerusalem was driven out of town and dispersed. Those who remained lived under the threat of arrest or worse as Saul threatened death to anyone professing to follow what was known as "The Way."

It would have been a horrible ordeal to go through. Yet, as religious authorities like Saul drove those Christ followers out of town, the Spirit orchestrated opportunities to proclaim the Gospel. Phillip, one of the murdered Stephen's fellow deacons, went to Samaria to preach to the Gentiles, non-Jews for whom a path to God had been closed off by the religious culture of the day. That entire community came to faith in Christ, hearing the Good News from a man who would never have gone to them but for the intense persecution of the church.

As Phillip continued his persecution-imposed travels, he encountered a servant of the court of the Ethiopian queen. This was a God-worshipper but also a eunuch, meaning they would never be fully welcomed by the Old Testament covenant community. The eunuch asked Phillip to unpack a difficult Scripture passage for him, allowing Phillip to share Jesus' message of grace that is available to all. The eunuch then asked to be baptized.

Upon returning to Ethiopia, tradition tells us the eunuch went on to share the Gospel throughout that nation, where a strong Christian presence continues to exist today. The early Christ followers submitted even their suffering to Jesus, and it became a platform for the Good News to be shared across the world.

Understand that, as unique as you are as an image bearer of God and a co-heir with Christ, your life is not the treasure. The hope you carry and the calling to help Jesus change the world is the treasure. The true, full, and authentic life you will provoke around you as you embrace the danger of difference is the treasure.

In his second letter to the Corinthian church, Paul writes that we carry a "treasure in clay pots."[50] The fragility of life according to the world's values and priorities will leave you crushed, abandoned, distressed, and ultimately on your own. But because you carry the hope of Jesus, and because the same power that raised Jesus from the dead lives inside of you, you can embrace the danger of difference and face persecution of all kinds.

To be clear, I am not suggesting you go looking for persecution. Jesus calls you to provoke life, which is enough to help Him change the world. In a world where Christianity no longer has privileged status, intentionally provoking persecution will harm the perception of Jesus. Enough harm has already been done because of the actions of Christians. While you are free in Christ, you are not free to be a jerk. There are far too many of our siblings in Christ who have apparently missed that message.

Paul offers a compelling vision for life in a pluralistic society in his letter to the Romans.[51] The church in Rome was significantly more marginalized than what we see in America, but the instructions he gives are still relevant. He tells the Roman Christians to show sincere love and honor - a stark contrast to the insincerity and manipulative culture of the city. They were to be generous, firm in their foundation in Christ, and inclusive of anyone who came to them regardless of societal status.

There should not have been the popular, the persecuted, and those in between among the Body of Christ. Paul wanted them to pursue peaceful relations with those in the city. When conflict, harassment, and persecution would come, vengeance would be left to God, and goodness would overcome evil.

By adopting this stance, the Church in the first century became a haven for those struggling under persecution. What if the Church today could become this? Congregations can be a place not only of worship but of equipping one another to live differently. Members can stand in support of one another when those dangers become realized. The family of faith can welcome those crushed by the weight of systemic persecution, meeting them with the treasure of the hope of the Gospel. Together, you and I can stoke the fire of love for God and the community that will compel us to embrace the danger of difference.

As a parent, I feel the heavy burden to keep my children safe and to present the world to them as a safe place. I can only imagine the burden God must feel as our heavenly parent. But the world is not a safe place. It is marred by sin and evil. There are spiritual and systemic forces at play that seek to deny life, whether it by physical life or the true, full, authentic life Jesus came to bring.

It is those most vulnerable to life being denied who need the Church to stand with them with a posture of love, not anger or vengeance. The "bully" is just as much a child of God as his victim. That does not excuse the bully's behavior, nor does it mean that behavior should be permitted to continue, but it does inform our stance against that behavior.

Your embracing the danger of difference with a posture of love provokes life because it reflects the very character of Christ, who humbly surrendered Himself to the danger of difference. And just as God raised Jesus up, God will lift you from whatever the outcome of the difference you embrace.

The glory of God at work in your situation will attract others and motivate them to live differently as well regardless of the cost. This is how the love of Christ and the movement of the Gospel has spread throughout the generations and it has the power to change the world.

APPLICATION

What you can do: There are many positive ways to live differently due to your faith, but if you aren't experiencing either direct or systemic persecution, there probably is not much difference in your life compared to others. Spend some time in prayer about how your life can begin to diverge from the norm in a way that provokes life, then take action.

What your church can do: People struggle to embrace the danger of difference because there aren't many examples of how this looks. Find ways to tell stories of those who have embraced the danger of difference, either here in the US or around the world, and the persecution they face as a result. It would help if you also shared how other churches and followers of Jesus have responded to that persecution and perhaps look for ways your congregation can partner with persecuted siblings in Christ.

Discussion Questions:

1. What was high school like for you? Were you one of the popular, the persecuted, or somewhere in between?
2. When have you or someone you knew been persecuted or suffered because of a firmly held belief or opinion?
3. What would being persecuted for your faith look like today, and what would you have to do to be on the receiving end of that persecution?

Rejoice When There Is Resistance

Blessed are you when people revile you and persecute you and utter all kinds of evil against you falsely on my account. Rejoice and be glad, for your reward is great in heaven, for in the same way they persecuted the prophets who were before you.

Matthew 5:11-12

The start of the New Year is known for being the most popular time to join a gym. Motivated by New Year's resolutions and advertisements featuring svelte fitness trainers and discounts on memberships, Americans flock in droves to sign up and get their bodies moving. For the first two months, gyms are packed.

By March, they return to normal levels of utilization. Why? Because working out is hard. You wake up sore the day after going, and the second day of recovery is even worse. The excitement of "New Year, New You" gives way to the realization that physical fitness is a grind. It takes a lot of time and consistency before you begin to see results. In a culture that seeks comfort over challenge and immediate gratification over patient accomplishment, it just feels easier to stay home.

I know this because I've done this—*a lot.* I've joined gyms, hired trainers, and investigated a variety of workouts. I abandoned those efforts many times as the grind of adding a discipline to my already busy life wore me down and wore me out. The challenge was always compounded by the feelings of guilt that invariably come whenever a resolution is forsaken.

Along the way, however, I learned that real change didn't begin with physical activity. What needed to change first was my mind. I had to think differently about the pursuit of physical fitness and both the internal and external resistance to that pursuit I faced.

This culture has trained you and me to see resistance as a sign that we are doing something wrong. Parents use the resistance of scolding and grounding to eliminate behaviors and attitudes they don't like in their children. Teachers point to a lack of studying and preparation, and therefore discounting other factors, as the reason students score poorly on tests. The legal system limits the movements of accused criminals by placing them in jail or under probation restrictions when laws are broken.

You and I live under the cultural paradigm that resistance stems from you being bad or wrong and, therefore, should be avoided. But the reality of a life following Jesus is that resistance is a sign that you are doing something right and, thus, can and should be celebrated.

As you've read the chapters of this book, I imagine you've felt resistance bubble up. The way of life Jesus presents in the Beatitudes, the way of life that provokes life, is hard. It will require change in you, and that change will provoke equal and opposite responses from others. It will provoke life in some, but others will see the changes in your life and the changes you want to see in the world as threats to the status quo to which they have become accustomed and comfortable. They may resist you and what you stand for as a result.

In Luke 14, Jesus told the crowds traveling with Him how critical it was for them to count the cost of following Him and the change it would bring to their lives and world. He compared it to the building of a tower or the planning of a battle. In either case, if the architect or the military leader does not accurately assess what their efforts will cost them, they run the risk of catastrophic failure and public ridicule. There is a cost of being His disciple, Jesus tells them. To be His disciple and to help Him change the world, you must be prepared to surrender your life to His will and His wisdom.[52]

There are a lot of reasons the Church in America is declining, but behind many of them is that the Christianity espoused by many, if not most, American church members does not really cost anything. Christian Smith, a sociologist who studied belief systems amongst young people for a book released in 2005, coined the term "Moralistic Therapeutic Deism."[53] In his interviews of over 3000 teenagers, he found that they had been formed in a faith that taught them:

1. God wants people to be good, nice, and fair to each other, as taught in the Bible and by most world religions.
2. The central goal of life is to be happy and to feel good about oneself.
3. God does not need to be particularly involved in one's life except when God is needed to resolve a problem.
4. Good people go to heaven when they die.

Contrast that with Jesus' call to die to yourself in Luke 14, and you can see that the faith that was passed on to these young people by parents, grandparents, pastors, youth leaders, and Sunday School teachers is very different than a genuinely faithful response to the Gospel of Jesus Christ. Moralistic Therapeutic Deism costs nothing and therefore provokes nothing. It promises a life of comfort and ease but leads to spiritual unhealth in the same way a life devoid of consuming that which can build us up ends up tearing us down.

Understand that you and I did not arrive at this moment of decline in the life of the American Church by accident. The Church in America has become dependent on a system of spiritual complacency and preference. We fought wars with each other over what songs to sing in worship instead of engaging in spiritual warfare united against forces of consumerism, individualism, and materialism. Rather than committing to spiritual formation in the likeness of Christ, we allowed ourselves to be formed by mainstream media and cults of personality. Because our Christianity costs us nothing, it has not given us anything except some vague assurance of life beyond this one.

In a post-COVID world, the failure to form disciples in the decades leading up to the pandemic has not created a situation where many feel they no longer "need church." COVID disrupted Sunday-centric Christianity, and while there were those who fought against government-mandated lockdowns, many other regular church attenders realized that their lives got along just fine without attending church. It would be easy to characterize them negatively for that realization. What church leaders need to examine is why it was so easy for so many to jettison something that they formerly had made a priority.

Perhaps the reason, or at least one of the reasons, is that what churches were offering simply was not very compelling or transformative. Attendance, volunteering, and giving were habitual. When the habit was disrupted, new habits formed that offered sufficient value that it made going back to the former habit unattractive. COVID did not create this problem. It simply revealed the problem of a lack of formation and accelerated the consequences of the church not paying attention to it.

The impact of this is multi-faceted, but to say it simply, we have failed to build the tower and we have not achieved the victory. There is ridicule for the Church beyond her walls because our lives do not reflect the words, works, and ways of Jesus. There is decline within our walls as more and more previously committed Christians and a massive number of young people see nothing compelling about what goes on within them. A resistance-free Christianity looks very little like the true, full, authentic life Jesus came to bring.

But there is hope. The Church can change and can help Jesus change the world. To do this, you and I need to count the cost. We must think differently about the resistance we will face as we live out the vision Jesus gave in the Beatitudes. Rather than seeing resistance as a sign to give up or that you are doing something wrong, Jesus calls you to see resistance for what it really is - a sign that you are changing and the world is changing. Resistance is evidence that life is being provoked, so you can rejoice when there is resistance.

When you start an exercise habit, your body goes through a process of change designed to make you stronger. The weights you lift serve as external resistance. That resistance shocks your central nervous system, and lactic acid builds up, creating an uncomfortable burning sensation and an internal resistance to continue. If you just listened to the discomfort, you would think exercise was the last thing your body needed.

But, while that is happening, micro-tears form in your muscles, which prompts most bodies to go into repair mode when you rest. God designed your body to repair itself to be stronger than before. With proper rest, nutrition, and hydration, external and internal resistance leads to a stronger body. Not only are your muscles strengthened, but so is your mind. You just did something hard and overcame it. If you did it once, you could do it again. Even soreness is a sign of the effect of resistance and the inevitable reward of better health.

Of course, there is such a thing as too much resistance. Lifting excessive weight, overexerting during cardio, or not respecting your body's limitations brought on by age, illness, injury, or genetics can do damage to your body. While the tired cliche says that "pain is just weakness leaving the body," pain is actually a sign that the resistance you are facing is traumatic and the activity needs to cease. As someone who struggles with physical limitations brought on by an autoimmune disorder, I have experienced firsthand the impact of too much resistance on the body.

The danger in addressing a Christianity that costs nothing is that we think costly Christianity means placing excessive burdens of legalism and demanding religious performance from ourselves and others. This was Jesus' criticism for the religious leaders of his day, along with their failure to live up to the expectations to which they held others. He said of the Pharisees, "For they tie together heavy packs that are impossible to carry. They put them on the shoulders of others, but are unwilling to lift a finger to move them."[54] It was a hypocrisy all too familiar in the modern church.

This is where the metaphor of physical exercise as resistance, like all metaphors, begins to break down. The resistance you experience in following Jesus is not about exertion. It is not about doing more, working harder, and getting better. It is about repentance, a change of mindset and direction. As the character of Mary describes her life in the dramatization of the life of Jesus called *The Chosen*, "I was one way, and now I'm completely different. And the thing that happened in between was Him."[55]

The resistance you experience in following Jesus is the result of alignment. When you align your life with Jesus, it serves as a prophetic witness to the world and will provoke a response. Persecution and true suffering for your faith is a sign that you are doing something right. The Kingdom of Heaven is breaking in. You are provoking life, and forces oppose you provoking that life.

The first Christians experienced this in Acts 5. Empowered by an outpouring of the Holy Spirit on Pentecost, they committed to reflecting the words, works, and ways of Jesus in full view of a culture that had rejected Him. Their shared lifestyle attracted many and drew the ire of the religious authorities, who saw a threat to the nation's religious purity and their own power and privilege. They threw the apostles prison in an attempt to cut off the "head of the snake," or giving a talk on success. He was at a charity fundraising dinner, and the guest speaker asked the crowd for one person to step up and make a $1 million contribution.

The businessman described looking around the room, seeing looks on the faces of those in the audience, and then looking into his own heart. One person did step up and make that contribution, but he could tell everyone else, including himself, wished they were in a position to say yes to that ask. Like those at the dinner that night, we all want to be a part of greatness at whatever scope and scale we might join. Being part of something great means we will experience resistance.

Faith is the most basic way you can be a part of helping Jesus change the world. But faith is not merely an intellectual acceptance of the Gospel message. Faith, as the author of Hebrews defines it, is seeing what we hope for becoming a reality and the evidence of what we do not yet see.[56] James wrote that faith is not really faith unless it is accompanied by action[57], and action in the direction of the Kingdom of God will provoke resistance. That resistance is evidence that, while we do not yet see the fullness of the Kingdom breaking in, it is coming. If that were not so, nothing and no one would want or need to resist. That's how we can rejoice in the resistance.

Not everyone wants the world to change. You might even run into other religious people who are more committed to the status quo than to God's Kingdom. In Luke 4, Jesus went to His home synagogue to preach. He announced that what they waited their whole lives for and what their people had waited on for hundreds of years was happening. The good news would be preached to the poor. Prisoners would be released. Those without sight would see, and those oppressed would be set free. The year of the Lord's favor had begun.[58]

What should have been a moment of rejoicing morphed quickly into skepticism and anger as Jesus' listeners considered the One making these claims. Jesus was born in a backwater town to a family without social position. The idea that the Messiah would come from such a situation was ludicrous. As Jesus continued to speak, He proclaimed that this year of the Lord's favor would extend to the nation that believed God chose them and to all the world, even the hated Gentiles. In the end, they wanted to throw Him off a cliff.

The emotional attachment many have to their understanding of God, their practice of faith, and their belief of who is in and is not is difficult to overcome. If change were easy, people wouldn't fear it.

Not everyone fears change, but many do. There will always be pioneers and early adopters who drive the change or get on board as it leaves the station. Some are resistant to change, and their resistance can be fierce. They might insult, harass, and speak poorly or falsely about you. I've known more than one pastor called to a church desperate for growth, only to turn on that pastor when they begin to make the necessary changes that would facilitate growth. Rather than attacking the pastor for pursuing the mandate given, change-resistant segments of the congregation invent offenses and exaggerate character flaws.

I'm certainly not advocating that anyone facing significant resistance in an abusive environment remain where they are indefinitely. Again, there is such a thing as too much resistance or the wrong kind of resistance, and that does damage. But it is important to remember a couple of considerations.

First, resistance is not a new phenomenon. Many who raise the bar or call for change from the status quo find themselves on the receiving end of resistance. Heck, those holding both religious and governing power conspired to kill Jesus because He threatened the social order of the day. In our hyperfocus on His atoning work on the Cross, we forget that Jesus made many powerful enemies. You might, too.

Second, without the right kind of resistance, there is no change or growth. Nothing gets provoked. Resistance, both external and internal, to you who are embodying the values of Jesus, is a sign that your small part of the world is changing. If you are genuinely provoking life, there will be support and resistance. Leaning into that support and enlisting those who offer it to join in leading change can help you sustain amid resistance.

Of course, there will be times when the resistance is overwhelming, and you are forced to flee. This happened to Elijah in 1 Kings 19. While he had experienced a great victory through the demonstration of the Lord's power and the slaughtering of the idolatrous prophets of Ba'al on Mt. Carmel, Elijah's actions had placed an imaginary target on his back. Queen Jezebel swore that she would take his life by the next day.

Fleeing the resistance of this threat, Elijah finds himself alone in a cave. The word of the Lord came to Elijah and asked what he was doing there. Elijah explained his plight, to which the Lord instructed Elijah on how he might discern the Lord's presence. The Lord promised to show up, but not through a thundering earthquake, a mighty wind, or a consuming fire. Instead, Elijah would discover the Lord's will in a small whisper.

When the resistance you face is overwhelming, it is natural to want God to deliver you through some eruptive demonstration of power. More often than not, God does not work in the overt but in the covert. God does not speak in booming audibles but in a still, small voice. God's deliverance for Elijah was to provide him with his next best step and promise that he was not alone. Not only was God with him, but there were 7000 faithful Israelites who would have his back.

God will never lead you into resistance where there is not also the presence of support. Like Elijah, you may not see the support initially, but as you commit to provoking life and helping Jesus change the world, others are ready and waiting to support you. Even though they may not know it yet, God will activate them to come alongside you.

You may not know how God will fulfill this promise, but the promise is still trustworthy because showing up for those who carry God's name is what God does. The prophets, Jesus, and the early church all faced resistance but experienced God's deliverance and the support of a community, and that means you and I can count on this, too.

We don't rejoice when there is resistance because we are seeking out punishment. We rejoice when there is resistance because the presence of resistance creates an expectation of breakthrough when we suffer for the name of Jesus. And not only do you get to be part of the Kingdom of God breaking in and changing the world in this life but you will also be rewarded in the life to come.

Sometimes you will face resistance because you are provoking life and the resistance is merely the equal and opposite reaction to that. When the resistance you face comes from those already marginalized by Christianity and who suffer under the weight of various worldly injustices, you must take a second look at your efforts and what they are accomplishing. Jesus said that a tree is known by its fruit. What is the fruit you are producing? Is it provoking life or confusion, despair, or grief? Other times, you face resistance because, while you think you are serving God, you are actually advancing some different agenda that has co-opted God for its purpose.

The way to know is to observe where the resistance is coming from. Provoking life will lead to resistance from the same people who resisted the prophets, Jesus, and the early church: the religious, the powerful, and those committed to the status quo. They are the ones who in reality have something to lose when the world changes, and they won't permit that change without a fight. When your resistance comes from those quarters, that is when you can rejoice.

And if you aren't facing resistance for your faith in Christ, perhaps you have not yet taken a bold enough step of faith. This is nothing to be ashamed of because you aren't alone. Most American Christians have bought into the complacent faith of Moralistic Therapeutic Deism. Most aren't acting boldly. Most aren't provoking life.

But now is the time. The world needs you to get in the game. Jesus wants you to help Him change the world. And, if you are being honest, deep down within you is a desperation for real, true, authentic life. To receive it for yourself and to provoke it in others, you will face resistance, but breakthrough is coming. A rocket uses most of its fuel in the seconds following take-off as it encounters the resistance of gravity. That resistance only lasts until it breaks through the atmosphere. The presence of resistance to you living a life aligned with Jesus is cause for rejoicing, because it is a sign that the breakthrough of God's Kingdom is not far off.

APPLICATION

What you can do: The Beatitudes provide ideas for where to start in helping Jesus change the world. Pick the one you most resonate with or is most relevant in your life and begin to serve others in the way Jesus intended.

What your church can do: I believe Jesus intended the Beatitudes to be the principal values of those who were His disciples. As such, it is the task of congregations to form people in the values of the Beatitudes, not just draw the biggest crowds they can. Living out these values will create resistance and even drive some people away. Is your congregation ready for that? What would it look like for your church to take on a mission to provoke life by embodying these words of Jesus? Consider what steps you need to take and devise a plan of action.

Discussion Questions:

1. What is the worst insult you've ever heard someone say, either to you or someone you know?
2. How do you typically respond when you face resistance? When do you press on? When do you give up?
3. Do people know you are a follower of Christ? How do they respond to you when you tell them? Would they know if you didn't say a word about your faith?

Final Thoughts

It takes audacity to believe that you can help Jesus change the world. It takes even more to write a book about it.

Much of what you've read was written in a local Christian college library, tucked away in a cubical near the Theology and Christian Ministry section. Hundreds of books and probably millions of pages written. Each had an author who, like me, had a Spirit-led burden to put down on paper what they believed to be true about God, life, the Bible, the Church, and the world. Most of those books looked like they hadn't been opened in years.

The likelihood that this book could end up in their company is not lost on me. I don't have any allusions or delusions that this book will change the world. The words written here aren't my words and the thoughts aren't my thoughts. They belong to Jesus because they were inspired by His words spoken on a mountain that launched a movement 2000 years ago.

This is not the first book written on the Beatitudes, and hopefully it won't be the last. What I wrote here may be forgotten in a short time, but His words will continue to reverberate for generations.

I know this because they already have. The Bible is by far the most read book of all time. In the last 50 years alone, it has sold almost 4 billion copies. In comparison, The Lord Of the Rings, published in the mid-20th century, has sold *only* 150 million copies. I don't believe there will ever be a book more impactful than the Bible because Jesus' teachings provoke life in ways no other publication has. As the prophet Isaiah wrote, "the grass dries up; the flower withers, but our God's word will exist forever."[59]

That's why I am convinced you can help Jesus change the world. Not only that, I believe that was the plan all along. The Story of God and us in Scripture has stood the test of time because Jesus wants you to find your place in that story. Jesus raised up disciples to be active participants in building His kingdom and for those disciples to carry on His work long after He returned to the Father.

That work has been passed down through the centuries to you and me, but that work has not changed. Jesus instilled Kingdom values in His first disciples – the values He espoused in the Beatitudes. Those same values are what He is calling you as His disciple to embody today.

If Jesus did not want or need help, He would never have called disciples and handed them the keys to the Kingdom. He would never have modeled for them His words, works, and ways and for His disciples to embrace. Jesus would never have commissioned His followers to be His witnesses worldwide, and He would not have sent the Holy Spirit to empower them to be witnesses. And He would not have given you the same Holy Spirit He sent to them.

He did this because you have a role to play in provoking life and changing the world. That role goes far beyond just attending church on Sunday, reading your Bible occasionally, saying a few prayers, and giving some money when you have it. Your role is to take these Kingdom values, make them your values, and follow the leading of the Holy Spirit as you look for ways to live them out intentionally. You don't have to force it. If you are open, the opportunities will flow.

But you cannot go it alone. There are many "lone rangers" on the loose, trying to change the world on their own. When God works, it involves a community. Life cannot be provoked without the involvement of others. You were created in the image of God, and God is not a singular entity but a community, Father, Son, and Holy Spirit, who are distinct and yet whose existence is so indwelt that God exists as one. It is perhaps Christianity's greatest paradox, but you do not need to understand how that works to recognize that you cannot fully bear God's image without community.

This presents a challenge because a community can be messy. Congregations in this day and age are fragile. Many are dysfunctional, with leaders far more concerned with sustaining preference and institutional survival than embodying Kingdom values. There are GREAT churches out there, to be sure. Still, church shopping sucks, and leaving established relationships in search of a congregation that appears to pursue these values more intentionally is risky.

20th Century German pastor and theologian Dietrich Bonhoeffer talked about the danger of this in his book *Life Together*. He wrote, "Those who love their dream of a Christian community more than they love the Christian community itself become destroyers of that Christian community even though their personal intentions may be ever so honest, earnest and sacrificial."[60]

In your zeal for your community to reflect the values of Jesus, don't destroy the community that exists. You are to be a conduit for provoking life, including the community of which you are a part for as long as it is safe and sustainable for you to remain.

Because American Christianity has not taken seriously the values expressed in the Beatitudes and formed people according to those values, it is critical to start slow. Find a small group of close friends, whether they are from inside your congregation or not, and begin to reflect on each of Jesus' teachings in the Beatitudes. You could read this book together, discussing one chapter each week, reflecting on the questions posed, and imagine together how you might live out that particular Beatitude.

Of course, it is best to start small and slow. Begin in your own households, then as a group together, then in your neighborhoods, then through your local church. That's why each chapter includes ideas for how you and your church can live out the values espoused by Jesus in the Beatitudes, along with questions to prompt conversations.

Remember that Jesus is not looking for something *from* you, but wants something *for* you. It is unnecessary for you to strive towards these Beatitudes. Bathe your conversations in prayer, knowing that only the Holy Spirit has the power to change hearts and that yours is the first that needs to change. If you are open, the Spirit will show you the true, authentic life Jesus came to bring.

You'll begin to notice changes within you, including some that might make you uncomfortable. What you once prioritized in your life will seem less and less critical. You will become restless in any arena of your life where you've not previously allowed the Spirit to work through you. You will see your marriage, family, job, school, and friendships no longer as avenues for self-actualization but as places Jesus has sent you to live out His values. You will become far more interested in building God's kingdom than your own.

This is what the Bible calls sanctification. Sanctification is the act of setting something apart to be holy. Committing to provoke life and helping Jesus change the world sets you apart for something greater. It is a hard road and one not everyone will follow you down. But there will be those God will raise up around you. Pray for them to emerge if they have not already and give thanks to God for when they do. Seek the oneness and unity that Jesus prayed for as He prepared to go to the Cross in John 17: "Then the world will know that you sent me and that you have loved them just as you loved me."[61]

Above all, remember that, in the words of Paul, "it is by grace you have been saved, through faith—and this is not from yourselves, it is the gift of God— not by works, so that no one can boast."[62] God loved you, Jesus died and rose for you, and He sent the Spirit to live inside you long before you had any help to offer Jesus. Rest in the promises of God

FINAL THOUGHTS

in Christ, allow them to provoke life in you, and trust that, no matter how hard it may be to follow Jesus, He never gave up on anyone and isn't going to start with you.

Here is my challenge now that you have come to the end of this book: pick one of the Beatitudes and make it the banner under which you will live until the Spirit leads you to move on to another. Study other Bible passages that align with that Beatitude. If you need help, simply drop me an email at eric@provokelifebook.com. I created a Bible reading plan for my congregation to help them study all the Beatitudes, and that guide could serve as a jumping off point for your study.

Of course, don't just read the Bible. Be like the wise person Jesus describes, who takes His words and puts them into practice.[63] A life built on the foundation of Jesus' teachings is one that can withstand anything.

Even as I come to the end of writing this book, I feel like it's the beginning of a journey. I live under the same calling of Christ you do - to provoke life and help Jesus change the world. I can't wait to see what God will do, and I hope you will join me in this.

To continue this conversation, I will be launching an email newsletter, which you can join at provokelife.substack.com. I'll be sharing regularly the journey I am on to provoke life as an encouragement for the journey Jesus leads you on.

You are free in Christ to have the audacity to believe you can provoke life and help Jesus change the world.

What are you waiting for?

if need help or questions
eric @provokelifebook.com

newsletter - provokelife.substack.com

Notes

PREFACE

1 Quote appeared in the prelude to dc Talk's song "What if I Stumble?"

2 Galatians 5:22-23

IT'S OK NOT TO BE OK

3 John 2:1-11

4 John 8:1-11

5 Matthew 8:1-4

6 Mark 7:24-30

7 Mark 5:25-34

GRIEVE FOR CHRIST'S SAKE

8 From the website of the American Psychological Association: https://www.apa.org/topics/grief

9 Jeremiah 9:17-24

10 Joel 2:12-17

11 Romans 2:4

12 Revelation 21:1-5

13 For more information on the 12 Steps, go to www.aa.org/the-twelve-steps

LEAD WITH YOUR NEED

14 Isaiah 42:1-4, 49:1-6, 50:4-11, Isaiah 52:13-53:12

15 Isaiah 9

16 Matthew 3:13-15

17 Mark 1:14-15

18 Luke 4:14-30

19 Matthew 23

20 John 18:33-38

NOTES

21 Philippians 2:6
22 Matthew 4:1-11
23 Matthew 8:20
24 John 15:5
25 John 14:12
26 5Q by Alan Hirsch is a helpful unpacking of the five ministry roles in Ephesians 4
27 2 Corinthians 12:6-10
28 John 13:1-9

FEAST ON GOD'S FUTURE

29 Isaiah 55:2
30 John 4:34
31 Ephesians 2:8-10

BUILD A BIGGER TABLE

32 Colossians 1:15
33 Luke 10:25-37
34 Matthew 18:23-35
35 James 2:8-9
36 Matthew 5:40-48

TURN FROM THE COUNTERFEIT TO RECEIVE THE REAL

37 Philippians 4:11-12 among other passages.
38 Revelation 3:14-22
39 Revelation 3:20
40 The song is called "Sovereign Over Us." It is written by Aaron Keyes, Bryan Brown, Jack Mooring.
41 Matthew 6:25-34

WAGE PEACE BY WEARING LOVE

42 Isaiah 2:2-5
43 Colossians 3:14
44 Colossians 3:15

EMBRACE THE DANGER OF DIFFERENCE

45. Retrieved from https://www.forbes.com/sites/ewelinaochab/2022/01/20/one-in-seven-christian-minorities-under-threat-in-2022/?sh=9232a117d2d7
46. For more on this, check out the book *Baptized in Tear Gas* by Elle Dowd. In it, Rev. Dowd recounts her story of participating in the protests in Ferguson, MO following the 2014 shooting of Michael Brown.
47. 1 John 4:19
48. Psalm 31:24
49. 1 Peter 4:12
50. 2 Corinthians 4:7
51. Romans 12:9-21

REJOICE WHEN THERE IS RESISTANCE

52. Luke 14:25-35
53. Term that was first introduced in the 2005 book *Soul Searching: The Religious and Spiritual Lives of American Teenagers*
54. Matthew 23:4
55. Quote was taken from *The Chosen* Season 1, Episode 2
56. Hebrews 11:1
57. James 2:14-26
58. Luke 4:16-21

FINAL THOUGHTS

59. Isaiah 40:6
60. *Life Together*, pg 23
61. John 17:20-21
62. Ephesians 2:8-9
63. Matthew 7:24

Made in the USA
Monee, IL
24 January 2024